IRENE SOLÀ is a Catalan writer and artist, winner of the European Union Prize for Literature, the Documenta Prize for first novels, the Llibres Anagrama Prize, and the Amadeu Oller Poetry Prize. Her artwork has been exhibited in the Whitechapel Gallery.

MARA FAYE LETHEM is an award-winning translator and author. Her recent translations include books by Patricio Pron, Max Besora, Javier Calvo, Marta Orriols, Toni Sala, and Alicia Kopf.

'When I Sing, Mountains Dance made me swoon. Translated with great musicality and wit, it is rich and ranging, shimmering with human and non-human life, the living and the dead, in our time and deep time; a fable that is utterly universal, deadly funny and profoundly moving' Max Porter

'There's so much beauty in this wonderful polyphonic novel. Each page makes you fall in love again with nature, with imagination, with words, with life. When I Sing, Mountains Dance is timeless and unique' Mariana Enríquez

'[When I Sing, Mountains Dance] is fine-tuned to a kind of astonished and astonishing connectivity that's an act of revolutionary revitalisation up against the odds of any despairing' Ali Smith

WHEN I SING, MOUNTAINS DANCE

IRENE SOLÀ

Translated from the Catalan by Mara Faye Lethem

GRANTA

Granta Publications, 12 Addison Avenue, London W11 4QR

First published in Great Britain by Granta Books in 2022
This paperback edition published in Great Britain by Granta Books in 2023
First published in the United States in 2022 by Graywolf Press, Minneapolis,
Minnesota

Originally published in 2019 as *Canto jo i la muntanya balla* by Editorial Anagrama,
Barcelona, Spain

This book was translated with the help of a grant from the Institut Ramon Llull

A CIP catalogue record for this book is available from the British Library.

1 3 5 7 9 10 8 6 4 2

ISBN 978 1 78378 825 5
eISBN 978 1 78378 715 9

Typset in Arno Pro
Book design by Rachel Holscher
Offset by Avon DataSet Ltd, Alcester, Warwickshire

Printed and bound by CPI Group (UK) Ltd, Croydon, CR0 4YY
www.granta.com

To Oscar

Og þegar vorvindarnir blása um dalinn; þegar vorsólin skín á hvíta sinuna á árbakkanum; og á vatnið; og á tvo hvíta svani vatnsins; og laðar vornálina frammúr keldum og veitum, – hver skyldi þá trúa því að þessi grösugi friðsæli dalur búi yfir sögu vorrar fyrri ævi; og yfir forynjum hennar? Menn ríða meðfram ánni, þar sem hestar liðinna tíða hafa gert sér götur hlið við hlið á breiðu svæði öld frammaf öld, – og ferskur vorblærinn stendur gegnum dalinn í sólskininu. Á slíkum dögum er sólin sterkari en fortíðin.

Sjálfstætt fólk
HALLDÓR LAXNESS

And when the spring breezes blow up the valley; when the spring sun shines on last year's withered grass on the river banks; and on the lake; and on the lake's two white swans; and coaxes the new grass out of the spongy soil in the marshes—who could be-lieve on such a day that this peaceful, grassy valley brooded over the story of our past; and over its spectres? People ride along the river, along the banks where side by side lie many paths, cut one by one, century after century, by the horses of the past—and the fresh spring breeze blows through the valley in the sunshine. On such a day the sun is stronger than the past.

Independent People
HALLDÓR LAXNESS
Translated from the Icelandic by J. A. Thompson

CONTENTS

I

LIGHTNING

We arrived with full bellies. Painfully full. Black bellies, burdened with cold, dark water, lightning bolts, and thunderclaps. We came from the sea and from other mountains, and from unthinkable places, and we'd seen unthinkable things. We scratched at the rock atop the peaks, as if we bore salt, to ensure not even weeds would sprout there. We chose the color of the hills and the fields, and the gleams in rivers, and the glints in upward-glancing eyes. When the wild beasts caught sight of us, they cowered deep in their caves and crimped their necks, lifting their snouts to catch the scent of damp earth approaching. We covered them all like a blanket. The oak and the boxwood and the birch and the fir. Shhhhhhh. And they all went silent, because we were a stern roof and it was up to us to decide who would have the tranquility and joy of a dry soul.

After our arrival all was stillness and pressure, and we forced the thin air down to bedrock, then let loose the first thunderclap.

Bang! A reprieve. And the coiled snails shuddered in their secluded homes, godless and without a prayer, knowing that if they didn't drown, they would emerge redeemed to breathe the dampness in. And then we poured water out in colossal drops like coins onto the earth and the grass and the stones, and the mighty thunderclap resounded inside the chest cavity of every beast. And that was when the man said damn and blast. He said it aloud, because when a man is alone there's no need to think in silence. Damn and blast, you had to get yourself stuck in a storm. And we laughed, huh, huh, huh, huh, as we dampened his head, and our water slunk into his collar, and slid down his shoulder and the small of his back. Our droplets were cold and made him cross.

The man came from a house not far off, halfway up to the crest, by a river that must have been cold because it hid beneath the trees. There he'd left behind two cows, a bunch of pigs and hens, a dog and two roving cats, an old man, and a wife and two kids. Domènec was the man's name. And he had a lush midmountain garden patch and some poorly plowed fields beside the river. The patch was tended by the old man—his father, whose back was flat as a board—and Domènec plowed the fields. Domènec had come to reel off his verses over on this side of the mountain. To see what flavor and what sound they had, because when a man is alone there's no need to whisper. That evening when he checked on the herd he found a fistful of early black chanterelles, and he carried the mushrooms wrapped in the belly of his shirt. The baby cried when he left the house, and his wife said "Domènec" as if protesting, as if pleading, and Domènec went out anyway. It's hard to come up with verses and contemplate the

4

virtue hidden inside all things when the kids are crying with the shrillness of a flayed piglet, making your heart race despite your best efforts to keep calm. And he wanted to go out and look at the cows. He had to go out and look at the cows. What did Sió know about cows? Nothing. The calf went maaaaaaaaaaa, maaaaaaaaaaaaaaa. Desperately. Sió knew nothing about cows. And again he cried out, damn and blast!, because we'd snuck up quickly, hell yes, capricious and stealthy, and we'd trapped him. Damn and blast!, because the calf's tail was stuck in a jumble of wires. The wires had gotten lodged between two trees, and what with all its straining the calf's legs were shredded and gleamed bloody, ragged and dirty. It went maaaaaaaaaaa, maaaaaaaaaaaa, trapped by its tail between the two trees, and its mother guarded it restlessly. Through the downpour Domènec climbed over to the animal. His legs were good and strong from barreling up the mountain to get some air when the kids were yelling too much, or when they weighed too heavy on him, and the plowing weighed too heavy on him, and the old man's silence, and all the words, one after the other, from his wife, who was called Sió, and who was from Camprodon, and who'd gotten herself into a fine fix, agreeing to go up there to that mountaintop with a man who slipped away and an old man who never spoke. And of course, sometimes Domènec loved her, loved her fiercely, still. But what a weight, for the everlasting love of God and Satan, how heavy that house could be! Folks should have more time to get to know each other before they marry. More time to live before making children. Sometimes he grabbed her by the waist and spun her around, round and round, like when they were courting, because Sió, oh Sió, lord have mercy, what a pair of legs! He dropped the

5

chanterelles. The calf lowed. Domènec approached the animal, leading with his hands. Slowly, step by step. Saying things in a deep, quieting voice. Ssssh, ssshh, he said. Its mother watched him warily. Domènec's hair was streaming wet. When he got home he'd have Sió heat up some water to wash off the cold and the rain. He looked at the wire that cut into the calf's legs every time it moved. He grabbed its tail firmly, pulled out his knife, and deftly cut the knot. And then we let loose the second bolt. Quick as a snake. Angry. Wide like a spiderweb. Lightning goes where it wants to, like water and landslides and little insects and magpies, transfixed by all things pretty and shiny. The knife was out of Domènec's pocket and it gleamed like a treasure, like a precious stone, like a fistful of coins. The metal blade, polished mirror, reflected us back. Like open arms, luring us closer. Lightning goes where it will, and the second bolt went into Domènec's head. Deep, deep down, down to his heart. And everything he saw inside his eyes was black from the burn. The man collapsed onto the grass, and the meadow pressed its cheek to his, and all our giddy, happy waters moved into him through his shirtsleeves, beneath his belt, into his underwear and socks, searching for still-dry skin. He died. And the cow took off in a frenzy, and the calf followed after.

The four women who'd witnessed it approached him. By degrees. Because they weren't used to taking any interest in how people die. Or in attractive men. Or in ugly men, for that matter. But the scene had been captivating. The light so bright and so dazzling that it sated all need for seeing. The knife had called to the lightning, the lightning had hit the man's head, bull's-eye, it had parted his hair right down the middle, and the cows had fled in a frenzy, like in some slapstick comedy. Someone should write a song about the man's hair and the lightning comb. Putting pearls in his hair, in the song, white like the gleam off the knife. And include something about his body, and his open lips, and his light eyes like cups filling up with rain. About his face, so lovely on the outside and so burned on the inside. And about the torrential water that fell onto his chest and rushed beneath his back, as if it wanted to carry him off. And about his hands, the song would tell, stumpy and thick and calloused, one open like a flower expecting a bee, the other gripping the knife like tree roots swallowing a rock.

One of the women, the one named Margarida, touched his hand, partly to find out if the man was burning with the lightning bolt inside him, and partly just for the caress. Then the women left him be and gathered up the soaking wet black chanterelles he'd dropped, and abandoned the scene, because they had many other things to do, and many other things to think about. Then, as if their satisfaction were contagious, we stopped raining. Sated. Dispersed. And when it was clear we were done, the birds hopped out onto the branches and sang the song of the survivors, their little stomachs filled with mosquitoes, yet bristling and furious with us. They had little to complain about, as we hadn't even hailed, we'd rained just enough to kill a man and a handful of snails. We'd barely knocked down any nests and hadn't flooded a single field.

We retreated. Dog-tired. And we looked upon our work. Leaves and branches dripped, and we headed off, vacant and slack, for elsewhere.

One time we rained frogs and another time we rained fish. But best of all is hail. Precious stones pummel towns and skulls and tomatoes. Round and frozen. Covering terraced walls and paths with icy treasure. The frogs fell like a plague. The men and women ran, and the frogs, who were teensy-weensy, hid. Alas. The fish fell like a blessing on the men and women's heads, like slaps, and the people laughed and lifted the fish up in the air as if they wanted to give them back to us, but they didn't want to and we wouldn't have wanted them back anyway. The frogs croaked inside our bellies. The fish stopped moving but didn't die. But whatever. Best of all are the hailstorms.

THE NAMES OF THE WOMEN

Eulàlia did tell them how the Great He-Goat's anus was so soft, tender as a newborn's from how we coddled and kissed it, and how his shaft was cold as an icicle, and I laughed and laughed and laughed, and all that laughing 'twere what got me hanged. 'Twas that laughter, like a heady venom inside me, like the witch milk from a spurge, 'tis why I remember all the things. Because the laughter was white and contagious like tickles there inside my blood and if you broke my arm, white milk would come out instead of red blood. And the laughter left me emptied. They could've saved themselves the trouble of the tortures and the rooms that stank of piss, could've saved those ropes that stretched out so long, and the wool rags full of ash, and their waiting for me to stop laughing and confess. Confess what? Laughing was a good thing, 'twas a cushion, 'twas like eating a pear, like sticking your feet into a waterfall on a summer's day. I ne'er would've stopped laughing for all the gold in the world, not for all the hurt in the world. The laughter unhitched me from the arms and legs and hands what'd been my loyal companions till then, and from the skin I'd covered and uncovered so many times, and it washed away the pain and grief over things that men can do to you. It done emptied me out like a dunderhead, all that heeheeheehee and hahahaha, and my noggin went clong-clong with the whistling air that entered me and came out my nose and ears. The laughing left my little head clean as a walnut shell, fit to hold all the stories and all the things what we said we done, and all the things they said we done against God and Jesus and all the saints and the Virgin. What Virgin? A god like each of their fathers, evil, evil, evil, and a torturer like them, and frightened by all the lies they'd repeated so many times they done come to believe them. For there be not a single one left on these mountains, nary a one of those who did point at us, who locked us up, who searched for the devil's mark upon us, who knotted the nooses and tightened the ropes. Because staying or not staying had nary a thing to do with the fires of hell, nor with divine punishment, nor with any faith, nor with any sorts of virtue. No. Being able to get up every morn to gather penny buns and golden chanterelles and to make piss and tell stories 'tis to do with the thunderclaps what befall that tree and that man. 'Tis to do with the infants born whole and the infants what aren't, and the infants born whole but with their innards not in the right places. Has to do with being the bird what the buzzard hunted or the hare the dog hunted, or not. And the Virgin and child and the demon 'twere all fashioned of the selfsame folly.

Of us all, 'tis Joana the eldest. She did come from a house nigh mine, Joana did, and everyone did know she would make cures in a cauldron, and one day she bade me join her if I so desired to learn, and if I desired to go along with her at night. And to have her teach me how to cure fevers, and inflict the evil eye and goiters, and nursling maladies and wounds and cattle diseases. And to find lost and stolen objects and cast glances. Oh, such innocence. For ere our biggest sin against God 'twas getting up every morn after they hanged us, and gathering flowers and eating blackberries.

They all left Joana be and they all did call for her when they went into labor or suffered goiters. Until that time when the hail fell heavy. Joana kept a field of wheat, and when the hail razed all the other fields, nary a hailstone fell on hers. They did say 'twas Joana had made the storm with some of her powders. Sorceress! they did yell. And then the son of her neighbor, who was called Little Joan, a five-year-old lad who was just about the first to call her sorceress, fell ill and his feet did swell purple and black, and he did expire four days later, and everyone did point at Joana, and did exclaim that she had empoisoned his victuals. Get her, get that old strumpet, that sorceress! And they did. And soon after that, little, little tiny frogs did rain down, and Joana sayeth unto them that if she so desired she could bring on the hail, or bring down a rain of frogs, or make all their livestock die, and then they did take me also and Joana said nothing more ever again. But I was fine, for I learned to laugh.

And then Eulàlia did appear, from Tregurà de Dalt, and she did tell them how she had once gone to Andorra to unearth a dead baby and extract its lungs and liver, to make of it an unguent to kill people and livestock. And then she did tell of how she bound men so they could not lie with other women but only with their wives. Since she made six knots on the strings of their undergarments and then with every knot she did say, I bind you on behalf of God, Saint Peter and Saint Paul, and the whole heavenly court, and on behalf of Beelzebub and Tió and Cuxol, so that you cannot join carnally with any woman who be not your wife. And once, she bound a man and a woman, who were neighbors of hers and who were cruel and threw rocks at her. She did bind them with hairs from their heads, so they couldn't copulate. And when the husband wasn't there, the woman couldn't live without him, and when he was there and wanted to come close to her, her entire body itched such as she thought she might die, and she couldn't stand to be near him. And that way four years passed. Four years! Hahaha heehee. And then one day, their son who took care of their goats brought the animals past Eulàlia's land, and Eulàlia did say oh may bad wolves devour your goats. And right then and there, a wolf pounced into his herd and killed a goat. Then they took Eulàlia, too, and when they had her, she dared tell them that one night the four of us had snatched a nursling from his mother's side, and taken him to a field, and we had played with him as if he were a ball.

Eulàlia always did tell the best stories, still does, better than anyone. Stories that make me laugh, laugh, laugh, until something loosens up inside of me, even deeper inside than the little drops of piss. She tells stories, and we are there in her stories, and verily what a joy 'tis to be there in them. Inside Eulàlia is a little voice, deep, deep inside, what tells her tales, a little voice, the devil's voice, what told her about the misdeeds, and 'twas spurred on by the pain men inflicted upon her and unleashed like a tongue what no longer knows how to lie still. The little voice came from deep inside her own head, like a fount, springing forth with images and words.

"We entered the forest, I upon a black she-ass, and Dolceta from Can Conill"—"'tis I!" I exclaimed—"upon a fox, and there was no moon and the stars gave nary any light, and a branch leaped out into my path verily like a claw scratching my face, and I said, 'Jesus!' and I fell from the she-ass, and Dolceta said, 'Never say "Jesus" again.' And I paid her mind. We did go to the Roca de la Mort, we did go there with our armpits smeared with an unguent that scorches the hairs forevermore, and that is why our armpits are bare. When we were there at the Rock, all of us, men and women, did mark a cross upon the ground and we did lower our skirts and we did each place our buttocks there upon the cross, forswearing faith and God. And then we did kiss the devil's anus, one by one. And sometimes he took the form of a calico cat and sometimes of a he-goat, and he said unto us, 'Art thou with me, my child?' and we all did answer yes. And then we ate cheese and fruit and honey, and we drank wine, and we all joined hands, men, women, and demons, and we embraced and we kissed and we danced and we fornicated and we sang, all together."

Margarida cried. She cried and denied everything, she cried and cried at the injustice of it all and sometimes she shrieked, and I told her, come now, Margarida, don't cry, all four of us locked up there in the same dark cell that wasn't even a cell, that was for holding livestock. And we made a good pair, Margarida and I, because I just laughed and laughed, and she just cried and cried, and sometimes the more she cried, the more her face contorted, and the more snot and saliva dripped from her, with her face all red and all swollen and all ugly, the more I laughed, and the more I laughed, the more she cried, and I told her, come now, Margarida, don't cry, and we made a good pair. Margarida denied every accusation, one after the other, and the only thing she would admit to was having set the table at night. Placing the tablecloth, and bread and wine and water and a mirror, so the evil spirits could gaze upon themselves while eating and drinking, and not kill her babies. But they only need one little thing to hang you anyway.

When Eulàlia told them that Joana was the mastermind who did bring the ghosts and did make the unguents we smeared ourselves with, and was the finest at making elixirs throughout the whole country, and all the other wicked things that witches do, and that she was the mistress of the he-goat of Biterna, and that we were all three her disciples, Joana didn't even blink. Eulàlia didn't say that with evil intent, nor did Joana bear her any bitterness for it, when we were all done for. For she only done said it 'cause she ran at the mouth, just as all the air burst forth from my mouth in haahaas and heehees, and Margarida just cried and cried. All four of us there upon the selfsame soiled hay, covered in rats and fleas.

Joana speaks not, she denies nothing, nor does she laugh, but she is still the leader and still the sagest and always finds the best strawberry tree fruit and the best mushrooms and she's the one who knows the most about abetting births. And she is the first to piss when we find crosses in the mountains, and to grind her netherquarters thereupon. And she is the first to crap upon the tree where they did hang us. She makes nice, firm turds and smiles like a mouse while she is squatting. And she is also the first to shit when we come across little chapels and hidden hermitages.

The tales Eulàlia tells aren't all about witches or about us. Sometimes the little voice tells her things about the mountains and the stones and the pools of water, and the birds sing her songs and the fairies explain fables to her, and I follow her like a little girl, like a lapdog, like a newborn sheep follows its mother, ready to throw myself beneath a horse, if need be, to get back amid her tales. Because she makes me laugh, that Eulàlia does.

"Once upon a time there was a Christian king of Aragon who had three daughters as lovely as the sun," she tells me. "Just as the king and queen began to think about marrying the princesses off, they came to realize all three of them had been courting, each princess paired with a Moorish infidel. I do so love tales about the Moors. Furious, the king locked up his three daughters in a very high tower so they could never again see their beloveds. But one night the three princesses did bribe the guards with a fistful of gold coins and escaped the tower, and all three, along with their Moorish lovers, did mount three horses and ride off into the Pyrenees, far from the Christian kings and the Moorish kings. On the third day, the king went to visit his daughters to convince them to cease keeping company with infidels and to marry Christian princes, and when he reached their cell he found they had fled and then in anger he did exclaim: 'May God's wrath fall upon them, wherever they may be!'

"And all at once the weather shifted. A storm of ice and snow surprised the six fugitives on horseback, a storm so fierce that it brought the lovers into an embrace, and all six were frozen solid, unable to take another step. And there you have them, one behind the other, embracing their beloveds, the mountain ranges of the three sisters, covered in snow," says Eulàlia, pointing to the mountains.

Or she tells the tale of a water sprite captured by some townspeople, along with a white tablecloth they took from her. "Poor thing. They locked her in a kitchen so she wouldn't escape. She was a small woman, who sat all day on a bench, looking out through the window without opening her mouth, as if she were mute or couldn't fathom human speech. But one evening, the mistress of the house where she was locked up began to make dinner, and lit the stove, and put a pot of milk for soup on the coals. As the woman bustled about, the water sprite did swiftly shout: 'Hurry, hurry! Your white milk boils over!'

"And the wife rushed over to the pot, and in all the commotion the sprite leaped up from the bench and escaped out the door. And they say that right before disappearing forever she spit out: 'Ye shall never know what yellow dock root doth bestow!' And she laughed the little laugh of a ferret, and still to this day the people of those towns haven't any knowledge of the many properties of the thick yellow dock root."

Margarida sometimes cries over Eulàlia's tales, she cries because a father turned his daughters into mountains, or she cries over the things they did to us, the wool and the ash and the red-hot irons and the chains and the bench and the weights on our feet and the red blood. She cries over her death, like all things that die. And I tell her, come now, Margarida, don't cry. And sometimes she cries, too, when a baby is born in the cave, and I tell her, come now, Margarida, don't cry. And after the storm she did cry a little, too, for that man, because he looked so handsome there in that clearing, she said. What a shame 'tis that men are so quickly consumed, and how other men cling to the empty bodies and hide them and bury them to avoid seeing what will also happen to them in time. And she did cry again when they came looking for him and they carried him off, and he never did return to keep us company. Instead they placed a cross there where the lightning drilled into him. They are always sullying the mountainside with crosses. But this one was small. And sometimes we would go there, and we would piss upon it, as dogs do. And sometimes we would bring yellow faceclock flowers for him, there where the man had been laid out, wet-a-beds, we called them, for laughs.

THE WHITE TABLECLOTH

My children are like flies, leaving a trail of shiny black shit wherever they go. Tic, tic, tic. You can follow the path. An open chest of drawers. The good chest of drawers. The one that was a wedding gift from Father and Auntie. Where I keep my beautiful things. The few beautiful things I have. Well tucked away. Nicely folded and separated by tissue paper. And with little bags of rosemary. One of the drawers is open. And the fabric and the papers are crinkled and placed any which way. I know before I have a chance to check, from the thickness of the stack, that the white tablecloth is missing. The white tablecloth is so beautiful that you can't eat on it. I flame up like a match, thinking that if I had them here I would yank on their ears so hard I couldn't be held accountable if I tore them clean off.

I neatly fold the cloth napkins, the tissue paper, and the runner, and then close the drawer.

"Where are the children?"

Grandpa Ton sits on the bench, very still. He never was a big talker, but now he hardly talks or moves at all.

"Out," he answers.

"Out," I repeat. *Out* can mean any place from here to France. "Would you like some water?" I ask, and he shakes his head.

Sometimes his hands, when he holds a cup and drinks, when he uses a knife, when he places them on his knees, will set my heart spinning because they're so like Domènec's. Other times I look at the old man, so silent, so withered, so sad and thin, and I simply can't believe he is Domènec's father. Grandpa Ton's mouth is all dried up. Like a raisin. Some men's tongues get stuck and just shrivel in their mouths, and they don't know how to open up and say nice things to their children, or nice things to their grandchildren, and that's how family stories get lost, and you no longer know anything more than the dry bread you eat today and the rain that falls today and the ache in your bones today. Sad mountains. Those mountains took Domènec from me. My Domènec. A lightning bolt went straight through him like a rabbit. Two months after Hilari was born. And that was lucky, I think. Because I didn't pass on the grief and I didn't infect him with tears through my blood, the way I would have if Domènec had died while I was still expecting. Then my son would have come out tarnished, blue. No. I cried alone. I cried all the tears God gave me in one sitting. And I was left dry, a wasteland. And Hilari was the happiest fatherless child in the world. The happiest fatherless children, the least orphaned children, those are mine. It's as if they didn't need a father. Lucky. But sometimes a woman feels like giving up on life. When lightning goes straight through a man like a rabbit.

When a branch pokes a hole in her heart but doesn't kill her. And then she's forced to live. The children cry and force a woman to live. The old man is hungry and calls out for her. The folks in town bring her green beans and zucchini to oblige her to keep on living. And she stops being a wife and she becomes a widow, a mother. She stops being the center of her own life, she's no longer the sap and the blood, because they've forced her to renounce everything she ever wanted. Here, throw them all away, all the things you've ever desired, toss them into the road, into some ditch, the things you used to think. The things you loved. And look how paltry, how measly they were. That man and that mountain. They make a woman want a small life. A runty life like a pretty little pebble. A life that can fit in your pocket. Like a ring, or a hazelnut. They don't tell a woman that she can choose things that aren't small. They don't tell her that small stones get lost. They slip through the holes in your pocket. Or that if they get lost, you can't choose new ones. That lost stones are lost forever. Throw out your heart, too, into the road, amid the mud and the brambles. Throw out your joy. Throw out your soul and hugs and kisses and your marriage bed. You must, you must. And now get up and look at yourself on this morning, so thin and so blue. Go down to the kitchen, and put food inside your mouth, and put it inside the children's mouths, and inside the old man's mouth, then inside the mouths of the cows and the calves and the sow and the hens and the dog. You must, you must. Until you forget everything else, with all those musts.

I didn't nurse Hilari. Because my milk was salty. And my son grew, like a flower, with thinned cow's milk and store-bought formula. And I scarcely even watered and pruned it, that flower. Your favorite has to be a child that comes out of you like a root. I love them, my children, despite my soul's limping. Despite the yoke and the despondency and the heaviness. Despite the fact that there was nothing in the promises I made, the promises they made me make, about having to raise them on my own. I wanted a husband, my husband, and then if they came, the babies, well, that was fine with me. But just the babies? Why would a woman want just the children? I barely got to taste him. Before I could lick the honey from his lips, they'd gone straight through him like a rabbit.

It was his hair I liked first. Then his poems. And then the more I looked at all the other things about him, the more I liked them too. His hands. His legs. His ears. And the wrinkles beside his eyes, like little tails. His shoulders. His voice when he whispered, like a lizard crawling up your back, "You drive me wild, Sió, so, so wild," he would say to me. That gaze like a spear, like an arrow. A head filled entirely with mysteries, filled with words. "What blue eyes you have, Sió, so blue that fish swim in them."

I was lovely, so, so lovely. The bluest eyes in Camprodon. And I knew it too. I was lovely like my mother, who was born in a house they called the Ravishing House because all the women in it were so lovely and ravishing. And she married my father and they lived in town because my father worked there as a supervisor in the sweets factory. But I wanted a man who loved the earth and who loved ideas too. A man who knew all about trees and plants and animals. My mother died when I was born from being cut so much, she was petite. But Auntie

Carme, who was my father's sister, and my father, too, they would always tell me, you're like a doll, like a doll, the prettiest of them all, and they bought me anise candies and bows and books and jump ropes, and I was never sad about not having a mom. My auntie would braid my hair and say, you'll find a husband and he'll love you very much and you'll love him very much, and I would ask my auntie what will my husband be like? And she poured more and more poison into my innocent veins. And my father, who said he couldn't remarry, because no woman would ever be as lovely as my mother. Only you, only me, Sió, the princess. And more and more poison into my veins. A dollhouse. We'll teach you to sew, we'll secretly teach you to read Catalan, we'll teach you to cook and to dust. What a rage Domènec flew into, the first day he took me up to the farm and I had never fed a cow. My father worked in a sweets factory! I had never touched a pitchfork. You don't know how to do anything! he shouted. What was I thinking when I married a girl from town instead of a mountain girl? Angry as a pair of pliers. But you already knew that, that I'd have to learn all these farm chores. What was I thinking! he bellowed. And I cried and cried. We'd been married for seven days and we'd spent six of them in France.

Auntie Carme told me not to worry, that I'd learn quickly. She was the one who made the white tablecloth. She had made it for my parents' wedding. And I did learn quickly. To lead the animals and dirty my shoes with manure. Because love makes you learn things fast. And then my father and my auntie Carme died the night I went into labor with Mia. They died of sweet sleep. The brazier smoked and from it came a fine fog that filled everything and gobbled up the air, and since they were sleeping, it snuck inside them like a poison and they never woke up again. And when Dolors Prim, the neighbor, sent her granddaughter Neus to look for them, no one came to the door. Since there was no response, they busted down the door and there they found them, each tucked into a little bed, sleeping like dormice. They didn't know whether to tell me or whether to wait until after I'd given birth. And was it ever long, Mia's birth, so long I thought they wouldn't be able to get her out of me. She was a tiny mouse, a teensy-weensy little mouse, when she was born. Then they left me be for a day, like a ghost who nursed with little closed eyes and a sleepy smile, and I held my girl on my deflated belly, with her tiny arms like the soft inside of a crusty loaf of bread, and Domènec was dumbstruck with it all. And then I said, Domènec, how is it that you haven't called for my father and my auntie? And Dolors explained that they had died a very sweet death, and that she had bid them farewell on my behalf. Since I was still befuddled from the lack of sleep, and from having a baby that was mine, that was ours, in my arms, it seemed very sad and not so sad at the same time. Like an exchange. Like a fact of life. That some folks leave to make room for others coming in. We named her Maria Carme, after my auntie. I was still on bed rest, so I couldn't go to the burial, and it was months before I could go into town, and then, when I did, it was as if my father and my auntie Carme had been dead for years and years, like my mother. I was so full with the things that were happening to me, with Domènec when he would say that our love had grown even bigger, even stronger, because of our baby. That our love had taken shape, he would say. That our love was an angel. A nightingale. I was filled up with the magic of milk. Like a cow. And with Mia's little open mouth, like a toothless fruit that suckles and suckles, and with the springtime that was nearing summer, and it had only been a year since I'd become a woman, a real woman, a married woman with every right to call herself a woman. A woman with a man in her arms, and now I had a baby daughter from that love, like a little angel from heaven. And sometimes I would think that I felt so little grief over my father and my auntie's departure because it was their time, it was the natural course of things. Because it was my turn to be the blood and sap of all things. Because only joy lay ahead, down a wide and sunny path with thick-trunked trees on either side.

When Domènec met me, he told me I was pretty like a doe, like a kitty, like a lioness. He led me out onto the dance floor and said, don't bite. And when it was time to leave he recited poems in my ear. Poems that spoke of a girl who was me. That spoke of all the flowers and of jealousy. Poems that built an altar I climbed, playful, and happy and open like a flower. Boy, could he dance. Domènec danced as good as he did everything. He had a way with animals and a way with people. I would have given him anything, if he had asked. Sometimes I couldn't take it anymore, so much keeping my hands on my knees. So much keeping my tongue in my mouth. My heart beat so hard, from all the fear and the desire for his hands. We courted for almost three years of Sundays. One after the other. Except for the months when he shaved his head. He shaved his hair off once a year. And you could see his entire skull, the whole noggin, even though, when we were courting, I never saw him like that. He would shear himself short, like someone pruning a tree, he would say, to grow back stronger. Revitalized. Ready to make new branches and fruit. Because he had such lovely hair, Domènec did. Gilded like wheat and cane. And a lot of fear around losing it. And then, when he shaved his head, he would lock himself up in Matavaques, which is the name of his house, of our house, close to two months, so no one would see him, until it had grown back in a little bit. Two months of the year, I would cry and cry every Sunday. And my auntie Carme would ask me why did you have to pick a vain farmer? Because Auntie Carme wanted a husband for me from Ripoll, or from Vic, a salesman, a pharmacist, or a factory supervisor like my father. But he always came back. New and gussied up and bearing flowers and smiles and poems about the sadness of solitude, and I would forgive him. I would forget all my grief and all my rage, I would force myself to swallow the bile and the bitterness like medicine. I, who for the last two months had done nothing more than imagine he was never coming back, imagine him with his arm around some other girl's waist, fallen off a cliff while chasing some cow. I looked at him with glassy little eyes, so shiny they shattered. I looked him up and down like a cat who wanted to eat him, full and resplendent, and I parted my lips in a moan so he would press his hand lower on my back, so he would yank me to his chest, and his strong arms would propel the joy out from inside me. And then one afternoon as we were strolling he said it, I was twenty-five years old and my heart lurched like it was being towed: "I was wondering if you wanted to marry me."

I am well aware already of the tricks that memory plays, of

the traps that snare my mind so I recall only the good things, of how it chooses the nice apples from the tray and tosses out the bad things—like peels, like horse chestnuts—as if they'd never happened. I don't know what hurts more: thinking only of the good memories and giving in to the piercing longing that never lets up, that intoxicates the soul, or bathing in the streams of thought that lead me to sad memories, the dark and cloudy ones that choke my heart and leave me feeling even more orphaned at the thought that my husband was not at all the angel I held him up to be. And that he didn't love me enough, as, in fact, no man ever loves enough. My body was so ready. So filled with fear and at the same time so filled with longing, so filled with love that pushed aside the fears, as if the fears were a bunch of bats. He made me walk ahead of him. Don't put your arm around me, he said. In the little hotel in Ceret where we had our honeymoon. Don't let the receptionists in the lobby know that we're newly married, they'll get ideas. They'll snicker. I couldn't care less, let them get ideas! I'll slap that smile off your face, he said. I entered the room first, and I waited a whole half hour, and then he came up, he had gone to the café, and he told me we would wait until the evening to make love. We sat and waited. I wanted to talk about things, I wanted us to hold hands, I wanted us to ride out the fear and the nervousness and the emotion together, but he smoked and was silent, stretched out on the bed, fully dressed, with an arm over his face, and if I stretched out beside him, he would get up. Then night fell—never had anyone ever wished harder for night to fall. And he told me, Take off your clothes, and I did what he said, and Get into bed, and as I took off my clothes and got into bed, he went into the bathroom and

I waited another half hour. Then he came out, fully dressed. He turned off the light, and I heard him undress and feel his way over to the bed, and he touched me in places no one had ever touched me before. He touched me as if he were entering somebody else's house, as if his hands had lost all their skill, and it hurt but wasn't scary, and I would have liked to see him, see his face so it wasn't a shadow that groped my breasts, that pushed my legs apart and stabbed at my insides. And I was all buttery, when I could be, when I wasn't frightened by his hands like claws in the darkness, his beastly panting. I was butter because Domènec loved butter.

We never talked about the nights, because he was ashamed of the nights. As if he wanted to escape them and couldn't escape them. That's why he liked Mia so much, because she was a little angel who'd emerged from our mud. But I learned. Shortly before I got pregnant with Mia, I learned to seek out the tickles. I learned to position myself in such a way that his coming and going rubbed me where it set me aflame. My body is a good body. A body that learns quickly. A body that soon gets used to things and that knows how to find the right path. And it knew how to take advantage of the thrusting, closing my eyes and focusing and trapping pleasure that way, as it came, small and gentle, like a bit of water slipping down into a hole, and bearing down on it and bearing down on it and making it grow, and channeling it into the ditch. And I could scarcely manage to abide the pleasure in silence. To grind my teeth together hard when the wolf-fart puffball exploded inside me. To hurry to make it grow and make it explode before Domènec was finished. And I already loved him before that, but after the pleasure, there in the sheets,

28

when he was already sleeping, all alone there with that warmth between my legs, with that cloudiness in my head, with that gentle breathing, so hot beside me, I loved him even more. I clung to him like a tree, like a baby clings to his mother's breast.

Eight years and I'm still not over it. This damn void won't fill with resin. Because I married the most handsome man in these mountains. The most beautiful hair in the valley of Camprodon married the bluest eyes. Domènec had the finest hair, finer than the hair of any of the women. When he took me out to dance at the Camprodon festival, everyone stared. When we were courting and he walked down on Sundays, splendid and sure of himself, with those legs of his, every soul in Camprodon envied me. I only wanted all of this because he was part of it. This house and this cold and these cows and the noises these mountains make at night. Love is a deceitful venom. When Domènec died I was left alone with two children and the house and Grandpa Ton. With all these weights on my back that won't let me die. That make me stay here. This stinking house that's impossible to get clean. This old man, cold as a corpse. Domènec's ghost. Memory heavy as a gravestone. A day doesn't pass that I don't think of him, that I don't see him, that I don't remember him, that I don't dream about him. And the children, who don't understand a thing, who can't keep still, or bring peace. Children should bring peace, should be a balm, consolation, compensation.

They come home as it's already getting dark. How many times have I told them I want them home before dark? What on earth could they want the white tablecloth for? For the love of god. I grab them in the entryway, each of them by an ear, as if I'd caught two mice, and I drag them shrieking to the chest of drawers. Like puppies. No point wasting my breath explaining. You drag them over to the mess they've made and you smack their snouts. So they understand. Mess; smack. Mess; smack. When I release them they both grab their ears with one hand. Hilari's always afraid I'll rip his ears off. Sometimes, from the yanking, a slit opens up under his lobe. I tell him not to worry, they're attached good and firm. They look at the chest of drawers and don't say anything. My patience sparks up like lit hay.

"I'll give your ass such a hiding you won't sit down for a week," I threaten.

"Mama, we didn't do anything," says Hilari.

"Where is the white tablecloth?" I ask.

Silence.

"I'll ask you one last time." My armpits and my nape and my throat and my temples are burning. They look at the chest of drawers and say nothing. Like they're guilty, thieves and murderers.

"The water sprites took it away," begins Hilari, in a whisper, the cracked and sad murmur of a wet dog, of a pussycat that's lost a fight. Mia looks at him, her eyes wide. In surprise, but also warning. Those wide eyes are telling him something. She's telling him to keep quiet. To not say another word.

"The sprites came into the house, opened the chest of drawers, and took the tablecloth?" I ask.

Lips zipped.

"Hilari?"

"We gave them the tablecloth," he confesses. He closes his eyes, desperate. He looks at his shoes, beaten.

"Shut up." Mia spits out the words.

My hand moves to slap her, but I restrain myself and instead I ask, through gritted teeth, "And where is the tablecloth now?"

"They kept it."

"Why the hell did you take the tablecloth?" I demand.

"Because we wanted to see the water sprites." Hilari's head sinks down between his shoulders. Mia looks at me like a stone. The old man is lying on the bench. And I'm losing my patience.

"You're liars, worse than liars!" I shout.

And I spank them. I grab them by the wrists and I stretch them out on my lap and I spank and I spank and Hilari cries and Mia grinds her teeth. I spank them harder, blind with rage and with grief over the tablecloth, over the lies, the disrespect, rage and grief over where everything ended up.

Then I tell them they won't be allowed to go down to the river anymore, and they won't be allowed to spend all day following around the Giants' son. It's all over until the tablecloth turns up.

"Do you hear me?" I ask. They don't answer. "Do you hear me?!" I repeat.

"Yes, Mama."

I send them to bed without supper, and I cry.

The crying starts like a small animal. Like a single cloud, like a thin fog in my chest. It starts like a tiny pain, like a slow swelling. Like a discomfort, like a small bone lodged in my throat, like a series of stones in my sternum. And it grows, little by little. My eyes get hot and damp, and the spring gushes and the pots boil over, and there is no stopping it. The water escapes from beneath so much rock, and so much fog. And the tablecloth fans the crying, like a bellows, huffing and puffing. The tablecloth. And the lie. And Mia saying, Hilari, shut up. And my hand spanking and spanking. And the loneliness. And the old man. And the withered love that is nowhere to be found. And I cry with rage over the old man who is not my father, for I have no father and no mother, and I cry over the lying children who are mine, over those children who should have been a balm, a sweet spring, good children who take care of their mother and adore her.

THE BLACK CHANTERELLES

The cap of one is the cap of us all. The flesh of one is the flesh of us all. The memories of one are the memories of us all. The darkness. Yes, the darkness. Like an embrace. Delicious. Protective. Welcoming. Like a falling. Nascent. The earth. Like a blanket, like a mother. Black. Damp. We are all mothers here. We are all sisters. Aunties. Cousins. Then the rain comes. We remember the rain. We remember it on our skin, on the dark caps of those who greeted it. Mmmmm, they said to the rain. Mmmmmm, and they drank it in. Before. Mmmmmmm, we said, mmmmm, rain. And we drank it in. We drank it in through the elastic trumpets we had then. We drink it in with our black trumpets now. We will drink it in with the firm, dark, open mouths we'll later have. The rain goes tic, tic, tic. The earth swallows it down. The rain goes tic, tic, tic. We swallow it down. The rain comes from places and knows things. It's comfy here, down below. It's comfy in this forest. On this patch of earth. On this patch of world. The rain startles us, with a fresh, renewed awakening. The rain makes us grow, makes us bigger. Sisters! Friends! Mothers! I am all of you. Good morning. Safe travels. Welcome. Welcome back. And then we emerge. We emerge. We emerge as we have so many times before. Now. Now again. Bit by bit. Bit by bit, bearing in mind the small, dark, soft, delicate hole we make in the black earth, in the green moss. Our first tiny tip. Bit by bit, bearing in mind the forest's progression, the millions and millions of downpours we've received, the millions of awakenings, of little caps, of mornings, of lights, of animals, of days. Welcome, sisters. We remember the forest. Our forest. We remember the light. Our light. We remember the trees. Ours, every one. And we remember the air, and the leaves, and the ants. Because we have been here always and will be here always. Because there is no beginning and no end. Because the stem of one is the stem of us all. The cap of one is the cap of us all. The spores of one are the spores of us all. The story of one is the story of us all. Because the woods belong to those who cannot die. Who don't want to die. Who won't die, because they know it all. Because they convey it all. Everything that needs knowing. Everything that needs conveying. Everything that is. Shared seed. Eternity, a thing worn lightly. A small thing, an everyday thing.

The wild boar came, dark mouth, wet teeth, hot air, fat tongue. The boar came and ripped us out. A man came and ripped us out. The lightning came and killed the man. The women came and gathered us up. The women came and cooked us. The children came. The rabbits came. And the roe-deer. More men came and they carried baskets. Men and women came and they carried bags, they carried knives. There is no grief if there is no death.

There is no pain if the pain is shared. There is no pain if the pain is memory and knowledge and life. There is no pain if you're a mushroom! Rain fell and we grew plump. The rain stopped and we grew thirsty. Hidden, out of sight, waiting for the cool night. The dry days came and we disappeared. The cool night came and we waited for more. The damp night came, the damp day came, and we grew. Full. Full of all the things. Full of knowledge and wisdom and spores. Spores fly like ladybugs. Spores are daughters and mothers and sisters, all at once. Each spore like a falling. Like a mother. Like a seed. Like a ladybug. Spores that have known every man and woman and every thunderclap and every boar and the pots and the baskets and the rabbits. Spores sleep beneath the dark, damp earth. Inside them they hold all awakenings. All the boar fangs. All the women's hands. Inside they hold the caps and the flesh and the memory. Sleeping, curled up, beneath the darkness, seeking out embrace. Making paths and making life and making mushrooms and memories. Darkness. Yes, the darkness like an embrace. Delicious, earthy, sheltering, welcoming, nascent. And the rain. Like a wellspring. We remember the rain. We remember it deep down, in the darkness that was the beginning. We remember it on our skin, on the dark caps of those who greeted it. Before. Mmmmm, they said to the rain. Mmmmmm, and they drank it in. Later. The cold rain. Mmmmmmm, we said, mmmmm. The warm rain. The mizzle, and the rain that falls in big, fat drops.

II

THE BAILIFF

I wave them goodbye. In no time at all, Cristina will show up with a grenade. With the first grenade. I wave goodbye to them. They cross the morning as if it were a field. I recognize them from a distance because I've watched them grow up appearing and disappearing amid the terraced landscape. Hilari, lanky as a reed, with long hair of yellow straw. Like his father. Jaume, the Giants' son, all shoulders, small, dark, round head. I greet the neighbors, the men, the farmers, with a curt, serious, respectable nod. But I wave goodbye to those two the way you say good-bye to children, joyfully and wholeheartedly, my arm raised and waving like I'm on the top deck of a boat or a bus. Bye-bye! I wave them off enthusiastically, like you would children, because, goddamn it, they still are children. Used to be, in my day, in our early twenties, at twenty-three, twenty-four years old, we were already men. But now, now young folks don't grow up that way. They smile. They raise their shotguns. Hair in the wind. Brown, green jackets. Mia and the dog aren't with them. I wonder where Mia is. Backs straight. Feet inside their boots. Bye-bye! I wave goodbye to them and they enter the morning, never to return.

Hilari is a talker who fills every space with words. He talks until the onions grow ears and the animals flee, sick of hearing his gums flap. But he has a good heart, no one can deny that. Not even Rei, a neighbor with a soul rotted to the core, who could easily say bad things about Hilari, the way he does about everybody else. That he's limp-wristed and a pantywaist, up and down all day with that giant. Who knows what he might say about the young man's constant chitter-chatter, and about his friendships. Instead he gives him baskets and baskets of green beans. I've seen them together, Hilari asking questions and Rei responding as if bad blood weren't his lifeblood. But all three of them have good hearts. Mia and Jaume too. But Mia and Jaume are both of a more silent type, more inward pointing, more sedate, and that's why they found each other and are a good match. They give each other a little humor and warmth, both so timid and aloof, and they love each other and seek each other out like two cats from the same litter. And Hilari prowls around them like the loud runt. I don't know why I spend so much time minding other people's children when I have two of my own, two girls. But they're good-hearted, and good neighbors, and easygoing, those kids, both of Sió's, from Matavaques, and the Giants' Jaume, despite how his parents are and wherever it is he's from, he always says hi and he's always polite to me, and show me the company you keep and I'll tell you who you are. That Sió is one tough mother and her children are kindness itself.

Matavaques, the house of Sió, Mia, and Hilari—Domènec

and Old Ton have been dead and gone for years—is right below ours. In the winter, through the bare tree branches, you can make out Matavaques, and the pigsties and the vegetable patch. Old Ton died in silence like a candle, from a cold to bronchitis, from bronchitis to pneumonia, still and quiet and without so much as a goodbye. Poor Sió lost Domènec suddenly. Right after Hilari was born, he was hit in the head by a lightning bolt.

Beneath Matavaques is the Grill Homestead, which is falling to pieces. Now they say that the owners, who haven't been seen for years, want to fix it up and rent it out. Who knows. It's sad how houses up here get abandoned. Rei lives above us. And above Rei is the town. All cramped and stuck together, those men and women in the towns. On top of one another, everybody arguing and fighting over that clump of earth and that other one, over some claptrap or another. I just don't get it, how people can live piled on top of one another like that.

Farther up, past the town, so high up they're not counted in the population of the town or anywhere else, live Jaume, the son of the Giants, and his father, not long since widowed, who comes down into town once a year if that much. Standoffish and peevish as a wild cat, just as standoffish and peevish as his wife, birds of a feather . . . Jaume and his father can take one big step and they're practically in France.

Sometimes I imagine the houses like stars in a constellation. The town's like the milk in the Milky Way. And when a house is left to fall to pieces, it's as if a dot in the heavens went out. Along the road we make a nice tail of Ursa Major, all together. The Grill Homestead is the lowest one down, then Matavaques and then the Prim place, our house, where I live with Neus and the kids, and then, higher up, Rei's place, so close to town that I almost don't count it in the constellation, and then the town, all twinkly little lights in the darkness.

When I was young they called me Mr. Prim, because I married Neus—Neus! what a woman—and she was the heiress of the Prim Homestead. Then we got rid of the livestock and I started working for the town hall, and now everybody calls me the Bailiff, even though my name is Agustí. That's fine by me, because prim means "skinny" and, well, with this belly, it comes off like a joke. On the other hand, the Bailiff makes me sound a little noble, like I've got an important job. And I like my job. It's not backbreaking. And every day it's the same thing. Nothing to do with the rains or the droughts or the dead cattle or their diseases and their diarrhea. My job as the Bailiff is to fix everything that has to do with the town hall and the municipal spaces and the roads that belong to everybody, pull up and chop down dead trees, clean up roads, maintain paths, and keep everything neat and tidy and easy-peasy, no problemo, I'm handy, a jack-of-all-trades, and I like developing ideas and trying things out. Roads are the best part of my job. Keeping the roads tidy, the shoulders clean, the trees pruned, the asphalt shipshape, the signs straight, the dirt footpaths well graveled . . .

Neus works at the fruit stand, down in Camprodon, and our house always has the best tangerines and the best oranges, and in the summer the best melons, and the best cherries and the best loquats when it's their season, and peaches so juicy you could just cry. And we have two girls, Cristina and Carla. The prettiest and cleverest of them all.

Surely now is when it sounds out. And the noise scatters

through the tree boughs. Now it sounds out, surely, and the mountain quickly swallows it up. The mountain, with all its layers of fallen leaves and damp earth and stumps, and boughs and stones, and with all the birds with open mouths, and all the creatures famished. Nothing, not a thing, reaches my ears. Not the small, quick, soft, round noise made by hunters shooting in the mountains. Not even a shiver of foreboding. Not a single hair stands up on my back. Not even the murky hint of something bad. Surely they pull the trigger now. It sounds out now, all at once. But nothing reaches me, as if the trees were covering it up, embarrassed.

Our house and Rei's house and even the Grill place look into the valley, but not Matavaques, being a bit more sheltered. The town, halfway up the slope, is a town of ups and downs, and faces the valley, too, and even the church looks out at the mountains on the other side and at the wide sky. The town is a good town, with fewer and fewer people all the time, used to be nine hundred of us up here and now we're down to about two hundred. But that's fine with me, it's more peaceful. Lots of folks leave the mountains and go down into the city or somewhere else, and then people buy the empty houses up here to go skiing. Or they let them collapse. But it's a good town. With its ups and downs, the squabbles and the stewing. Nothing that doesn't happen in other towns. The mayor's a good man, even though he's the type who wants to make everybody happy and always says yes to everything, and when it comes down to it, does jack shit. But people can be so envious, and you can't please all the people all the time. And if they don't take it out on you, they'll take it out on the next guy.

Far as I'm concerned, the best things about our town are the things we do together. When everybody from the scattered houses gathers in the square and for a little while it's like we're all friends. There is no summer festival here. Our town's festival is in October, and we eat chestnuts. And at Christmas we sing carols, and on Epiphany the Wise Men parade in. You're looking at the blond king. We get together in the springtime, too, with the cooking contest. The same folks always win, so nobody else even wants to take part, but Neus and I do anyway. And some years we get lucky and there's a gathering to sing havaneres, those sea shanties from the voyages to the Americas. In the summertime. I love havaneres, I'm a big fan. Which is funny because I couldn't care less about the sea itself. I'm perfectly happy up here in my mountains. No interest in flat ground. The beach? No, thank you. But havaneres, what can I say, I just love them. Those men singing of faraway places, of grief and women and longing, they speak directly to my soul. Every hair on my back stands on end, and my whole head fills with images of the sea and boats and distant lands and the sweethearts waiting at port. I like the sea when it's in songs. I'll belt out: "I love you, my love, oh, how I love you. I love you more than the blue of the sea, like the gray sky loves the gulls, like water, freedom!" I remember the lyrics, and when I don't, I just make them up as I go along. I sing while I'm working on the roads and no one can hear me, or if one day I'm feeling romantic and I want to make Neus laugh, I sing to her, too, and she jokingly calls me her salty dog.

Once Neus took me to Calella to hear havaneres, drink hot spiced rum, and eat grilled sardines. That was the only time I actually enjoyed going to the beach. I still felt out of place there, with all those seaworthy men and women who all knew each other. We were total outsiders, fish out of water. I liked it, but I felt a bit homesick for the mountains, and for our town, and for our singalongs. Those seafaring folks are made of hard flint, too, but it's a different kind of hardness.

Who knows whether, in fact, the shot sounds out now, with me here thinking about havaneres, and singing about sailor love and saltwater. The shot sounds out, like the bad things that happen in the world, but if they don't somehow touch you, it's like they didn't happen. Babies. You two are just babies. You have to *always* carry your guns with the safety on. Goddamn it. Life and the world and history and everything—they're all full of bad things that happen at the wrong time, in the wrong place, and with no one to stop them.

My father said he could hear the shots, in the mountains, when soldiers were executed. My father heard them, but today I don't hear a thing. He kept his mouth shut, out of fear. Out of fear they'd killed his brother. And his silence didn't do him a lick of good.

He was just a kid, my father, when a group of retreating Republican soldiers came by his house. They were holding a bunch of National soldiers as prisoners. They knocked on the door and they were let in. They grabbed cured sausage and cheese and salt pork. Then they told my father's oldest brother to come with them, to show them the way to France. And his brother blurted out: "You expect me to put my espadrilles back on now?" And they made him put his espadrilles back on, and once they were laced up, a soldier said to him: "This will be the last time you have to put them on." He showed them the way, and he never came back. My father heard the shots when they executed the prisoners and his brother. What could they do with a bunch of soldiers from the other side, once they got to France? It was their last chance to take revenge, to kill, to spill enemy blood.

Then, three days later, as my father would tell us, the Ifni Riflemen came through. The whole family was in hiding and quiet as mice. But my father had a sister named Teresa, who wasn't quite all there; everybody called her Treseta. When the Arabs knocked on the door, Treseta—angry that the other soldiers had killed her big brother—grabbed a pot of boiling soup that was on the stove, climbed up to the highest window, and threw it down onto them. The soldiers broke down the door and slit her neck with a bayonet. He was a real angry man, my father.

And then Cristina comes into the house with a grenade in her hand.

"Papa, look what I found," she says.

She's my youngest daughter and she's fourteen.

"Fer crying out loud! Where'd you get that from?"

"The river."

"And what were you doing at the river?"

"Throwing stones."

Throwing stones after school. Kids today.

"Get that the hell out of this house right now," I tell her.

"It's not going to explode."

"How do you know it's not going to explode?"

"Because I emptied it out and it has no cap."

"Why would you bring a grenade into my house?!" I shout.

We head out. We put it down on the ground in the middle of

the threshing floor. How could you bring a grenade home, bird-brain? These mountains are infested with them, with pieces of rifles and with bullets and grenades. How many meters around does a grenade blow up? Five, six, seven? We back away.

"Don't ever bring me something like this again!" I tell her. Not imagining the boxes and boxes of grenades, pistols, rifles, bullets, mortar, and even bits of machine gun that in the years to come she would stash away for me everywhere.

"Papa, it's okay."

What in god's name is this child thinking? Jesus H. Christ.

The local farmers have always found them around here, weapons and things that the retreating soldiers left behind. And you know what smart folks do when they find something like this? Do you know what your grandfather would do? You know what I've always done? Look the other way. And if there was no avoiding it, we'd cover it up with a rock. Stick it into some hole in a retaining wall. Toss it over some steep bank. That's that. You wouldn't want them to find it in your house. And the fewer run-ins with the Civil Guard, the better. For Pete's sake, child.

"What should we do, Papa?" she asks. We stand there in the middle of the threshing floor with the sun setting, the grenade on the ground, like an offering.

"Think," I answer. And when I've thought enough, I say, "I'll take it to the Civil Guard."

"I'll come too."

"No."

"I found it, and I want to take it to the Civil Guard," she exclaims, with such adult conviction that I ask her, a fourteen-year-old girl: "Are you sure it won't explode?"

"It's empty. It's an iron casing."

"Don't touch it." Holy hell.

I go over to the hand grenade slowly, my backbone damp.

"It's okay, Papa."

The light grows increasingly colder. The shot must have sounded out a little while ago, and now Hilari is dead, and Jaume is carrying him over his shoulder.

I pick up the grenade.

Again she says: "It's okay."

Holy hell. Grenade in hand, I set off down the road on foot, then veer to the left. The shoulder straightens and we have to skirt brambles. She follows me. I open the electric fence. So modern, the most modern of things, that electric fence. Modern but designed for the mountain. The path is covered in cow shit, with sharp rocks, and fallen trees on the right.

"What should we do?" she asks.

I don't answer.

We cross the small, rocky stream, and the field opens up wide before us. The boars and the moles have turned over the earth. The grass is high. The sun doesn't reach down here and the light is quite blue. At the end of this field there is a river. It wends down into the depths of the valley, loudly. The mountain again climbs after the river.

"Stay here," I tell her.

I walk ahead fifteen meters.

I lift my arm and throw the grenade. Far. Toward the middle of the field, which is green and blue and gray. It cuts through the air all round and rusted. And it hits the ground just like a fat rock. Soundlessly, onto such a soft bed. Nothing.

Silence. The birds continue doing their thing. The river slides on, focused.

The girl says: "You see?"

She sets off running like a dog fetching a stick, her gaze fixed on the exact spot where she saw it fall. She finds it right away. I feel foolish. Of course it didn't explode. But I couldn't allow a grenade in the car with my youngest daughter without testing it.

We climb the road back to the house. At one point she asks: "Will they keep it?"

I don't answer her. Neus isn't home yet. We get into the car, the sun has already dipped beneath the horizon. Very soon Rei will find Jaume all bloodied, carrying Hilari's dead body. Our car slides down the road. I know them like a song, the turns on this road. When we get to Camprodon, the night is not yet black, it's dark blue. We enter the police station just as they've gotten word. Rei called saying there was a hunting accident up in the mountains. That Jaume, the Giants' son, shot Hilari, from Matavaques, Sió's Hilari. Hilari has been dead for hours. It was fast. Jaume carried him down in his arms from the mountaintop.

They are all standing, the Civil Guard officers, when we enter. A group of five or six come out and get into their cars. This station's always been still, quiet, as if half-asleep and half-abandoned. Its flag waves over it, strange and imposed, having been sewn somewhere else. The smooth, sad walls, the gates of concrete and barbed wire to keep all things out, the small windows, like eyes that've seen better days.

"What do you want?" an officer asks us in Spanish. He has a moustache and the face of a heavy smoker, a face that looks like he spent his childhood and youth far from these mountains.

"We found this," I say, and show him the piece.

"Ahh, that," he says, taking it from me. "That's nothing."

"Can I keep it?" pipes up Cristina.

"Whatever you want, kiddo: keep it, throw it away . . ."

"What happened?" I ask, pointing a hand toward the commotion.

"Nada, un accidente," he says. Not a single hair stands up. Not even a teensy intuition. Not even a little piece of a scrap of fear. Nada. An accident. As if accidents were things that happened far away. Somewhere else. To people you didn't know. As if today could never be the day of an accident. Nada. Nada. Un accidente. He stinks of old man. Of rancid cologne. Of tobacco. Of rooms that need airing. That man, the corners of his mouth fallen and white, like a catfish's whiskers, again says that's nothing: sure, kiddo, you can keep it.

When we leave, Cristina says, "Pop, I need a metal detector."

"What do *you* need a metal detector for?" I ask.

"To find more weapons from the war."

"Don't hold your breath."

THE FIRST ROE-BUCK

It was very hot, and very dark, and very cramped inside. My brother and his long legs, me and my long legs, curled up like worms under rocks. And all the things that make noises, and all the things that have smells and flavors, and all the things we didn't know, and all the things we hadn't experienced and couldn't imagine, were trotting and leaping and moving out there beyond our mother's belly. Until the noises began. Our mother's shrieks, the barking, gruff and high-pitched at the same time. One after the other. One after the other, which meant something was going on. That meant it was time. The darkness no longer wanted us. Our mother's belly a cave that no longer wanted us. First my brother and then me. First the legs, then the body. Inside we weren't wet. Inside we were dark and hot. Outside we were wet. And our eyes didn't know how to see, because they'd never looked at anything before. Inside everything was dark and they didn't know they were for seeing. Closed and resting. Outside we were wet, and the air let us know we were wet. You're wet, you're wet, it said to us. And it was cold like a betrayal. Mother came with a tongue that was hot like memories. With a tongue that cleaned off the fear and the blood. With a gentle and persuasive snout that said, here, over here. Upward, upward. Over there. But our legs didn't know how to walk, they didn't know how to move now that all of a sudden they had all the space they could ever want to stretch out. Now that they saw the point of getting your body up and going places. Because there were places beyond that belly. So many places. My brother stood up. There were grasses too. Thin grasses. Grasses that touched your nose, grasses that touched your eyes and belly. I stood up. There was sky. Sky light and dark. There was night, which was like inside the belly but with air and without my brother. There were stones. There was milk. There was dung. There was the sun, which was light and painful. There were all the things. The ones that smell. And the ones that make noise. The ones that frighten and the ones that comfort.

And then our mother separated us, me and my brother. And she hid us. Hidden, you can hear every sound. I like the sounds but they scare me too. I stay still. I stay still and hidden when the sun is in the middle of the sky. But when the light is cool, I test my legs. When Mother comes, and the sun is already departing or the sun hasn't come up yet, she teaches me things you can't see from our hidey-hole, and with her snout she says, over here, over here, stand up, up, up, and I test my legs in places even farther away. She shows me the water flowing down, the water you drink like milk but cold. She shows me the delicious shrubs and the tender sprouts and the small, good berries. She shows me the trunks of the trees and the smell of poopoo and the smell of peepee and the smell of other roe-deer and she tells me to run, to run far, if I get scared, to run, if I hear sounds, to run. That I'm little and cute but not everything in this forest is good. What things aren't good? Many things. Other roe-deer? If you hear a sound you don't like. If you smell a scent you don't like. You run, run, these little legs of yours are for running. And then she takes me back to the hidey-hole. Keep still, keep still, she says. And I hear the sound of the bees seeking flowers. And I hear the sound of the little animals that live underground. The sound of the birds singing. The sound the water makes when it falls from the sky. The sound of my mother returning. The sound of sucking milk. And then, suddenly, I hear the scariest sound of them all. The worst sound, the harshest. The sound of footsteps, too loud. The sound of shouting, like shrieks. The sound that doesn't come from the forest but from a place I don't know, a place I've never seen.

The noises of those creatures drew closer and I heard them coming, coming closer, finding me. They found me in the place my mother had hidden me. And they shouted. And more of them came. They were unlike anything I'd ever seen before. They weren't roe-deer like my mother and my brother, and like me. They weren't bees, they weren't birds, not rabbits, not badgers, not spiders, not mice. And then they grabbed me with their paws, which were hairless and had a lot of branches. I wanted my mother. I wanted milk. I wanted them to leave and I wanted the smells and the sounds. But they picked me up. Pulled me out of my hidey-hole. I was afraid. My mother had said, you, run, you run. But I couldn't run, and they took me with them. They took me a long way into the forest, farther than I had ever been, so far that if they put me down I wouldn't know how to get back. They took me away and I was very tired. And I was very far away. And I hadn't run and now those shriekers had me.

They put me inside a place like a snore. Like a mother's terrible belly, where instead of being born you die. There was a painful smell, a disgusting smell, a mangled smell, there inside. And I closed my eyes because I didn't want to see more. I didn't want to learn anything about that ugly place without forest. Without trees. Without leaves. Without grasses, or tender brush, or berries. And they brought water, but their water stank. And I was afraid and I curled up and I thought I had to get away. Because curled up like that, with no hidey-hole and no mother, I clearly saw that I would die. I slept the light sleep of those doomed to die, and the shriekers who touch you even though you don't want them to touch you came back. They always came back. And they brought more stinking things. They stank of dung, they stank of death, stink, stank, stunk. I was so hungry. And so sad. I didn't look, because I didn't want to see anything, but I felt their claws grabbing me, and then I opened my eyes suddenly, and I saw trees there in the distance. This time I ran and ran, ran and ran, and I heard the shouts and the blows and the sounds, but I was faster than the shouts and the legs of the shouts, and I ran and ran toward the trees, because after the trees were more trees, and after the trees, more trees, and after that the forest.

When I was in the forest, far from those who carry you off and shriek, I filled my mouth with fresh sprouts and living water, and I filled my nose with all the smells, and my eyes with all the beautiful things, and I thought about my mother and my brother.

My mother and my brother, who I would never see again because I was too far away and I didn't know how to go back to my hidey-hole, where my mother hid me after I was born. It had been beautiful having my mother for a mother. And my brother for a brother. But I didn't need a mother anymore, and I could barely remember my brother. Soon I wouldn't even remember my mother. Because roe-deer need mothers only when we're born, and when we're little and have to learn. And we have siblings only when we're in the same belly and drink the same milk. But I don't drink milk anymore.

I thought I would search out a group of deer who weren't mothers or brothers or sisters of anybody. I would search out a female deer and we would mate. The forest would be my home. Filled with good things and edible things and protective things and beautiful things. And I would search out other roe-deer so I would be a little less scared. Because the fear had gotten inside of me like a disease. Everything scared me and I was always running. I ran and ran and ran and the fear was never-ending. I changed dens and slept the restless sleep of those who are afraid to die. But I didn't see bald animals that shout and have paws covered in branches until many, many mornings later, and many evenings, when I had already known females and the rut, when I had fought with other males who'd scratched at my trees, and I had defended the bit of forest that was mine, and I had lived with other roe-deer, and I had seen small kids, and the trees had gone bare and the cold had grown and the food hid itself and grew tough and hard to chew, and the water had turned cold and white and hard at the edges of the river. I was alone, one morning, and I was eating fresh, tender grass and it was delicious again, and I didn't want any males near me, I wanted only a female, I wanted the males far, far, far away from me, and I'd kill them if I had to. The air carried the scent of the morning, a scent with no flavor to it, like water, so good you can't even explain it, and it carried the sound of the branches up in the trees and the happy singing birds. And all of a sudden the wind turned, like a neck, and then I could smell it, the stench, the terrible stink of the bald beast thrust deep into the pit of my fear. And the sounds they made. But this time they weren't shouting, these ones didn't shout. And their whispering made me even more anxious. I lifted my head, and I put my whole back straight, bristled, on end. I wanted to know where they were and which way I had to run, run forever and never stop running ever. Run like my mother had told me to run when I was born. And then, whoosh!, I set off, like the clouds, even faster!, like the hares, even faster!, the forest moved beneath me, beneath me, the ground trotted, I ran so fast the trees stepped aside. And then I heard it. The sound. Bang. The most terrible crash I've ever heard, the most deafening, the most rending. As if, after that crack, all things must die. As if no sprout must ever grow, no bird ever sing, no water ever flow, no sun ever rise. A sound like a wound. I thought I would die from that sound. I would die with all the things that would die after that noise. I would die, because the sound had chosen me. Farewell, forest. Farewell, mornings. Farewell, birds. Farewell, sun. Farewell, roe-deer who is me. Farewell, roe-deer who are others.

But I didn't die and my legs kept running, and running and running and running and running and running and running and running.

THE SETTING

These mountains are sublime. Primordial. Otherworldly. Legendary. Epic.

Pyrene was the daughter of Túbal, King of Iberia. And Gerió was a giant, with three men's bodies joined at the waist, who took the throne from Túbal. Pyrene escaped into these mountains and Gerió set them all aflame in order to flush her out. He burned her alive, and Hercules covered her corpse with magnificent stones, creating a mountain range as a mortuary sculpture, from the Cantabrians to Cap de Creus. These mountains are called the Pyrenees in honor of Pyrene. That's how dear old Verdaguer tells it. The Greeks were wilder, crazier. Greek mythology has it that Pyrene was King Bebryx's daughter and was raped by Hercules on a court visit, after which she gave birth to a serpent. Then the princess fled into the mountains and was devoured by wild beasts. According to the Greeks, it was Hercules himself—after raping her and knocking her up with a snake—who discovered her body ripped apart by wild animals up in the mountains, and he named the mountains after her in tribute. Gee, thanks, Hercules!

This is the route of the retreat into exile. Where the Republicans fled. Civilians and soldiers. Toward France. It's a damp morning. I inhale, bringing all that clean, wet, pure mountain air deep into my lungs. That aroma of earth and tree and morning. It's no surprise the people up here are better, more authentic, more human, breathing this air every day. And drinking the water from this river. And looking out every day at the majesty of these legendary mountains, so beautiful it pains the soul.

I head up, toward the town. I left my car all the way down in the valley, at almost eight in the morning. I ate a stale sandwich and I haven't even had coffee. The last time I came up here, last spring, a local told me these peaks are cursed and that every ten years somebody gets struck by lightning. He said his name was Rei, the King, with his dime-a-dozen face, toothless mouth, and skin so dry you could hear it chafing when he rubbed his nose. "Watch out you're not the next victim," he told me. "Run through by lightning." And he laughed. Crested storm clouds gathered. "Watch out you're not the next victim." King of the nutjobs.

Emotions are more naked up here too. More raw. More authentic. Life and death, life and death and instinct and violence are present in every single moment up here. The rest of us, we've forgotten how sublime life is. In the city we go through the motions with our watered-down lives. But here, here you really live each and every day. As soon as the weather turns, even if it's just a gawky bit of early spring, I have this need to get up into the mountains, at least once a month. Leave it all behind and just spend a day in the fresh air. Sometimes with a friend, sometimes on my own. If I can ever buy a little house up here, an old farmhouse, a summer place, I'll call it Can Gentil. But it would have to be a farmhouse, because I can't see myself in a villa.

Up here even time has a different feel. It's like the hours don't have the same weight. Like the days aren't the same length, don't have the same color, or the same flavor. Time here is made of different stuff, and it has a different value.

An early yellow sun slips through the leaves of the trees. And I hear the river flowing happily. Once I step off the damp, sunken footpath and head up, I see a few scattered homes in the distance, on the other side of the crest. The mountains there in the background, they could even be France already, with Espinavell at the far end, and, my god, what a landscape. We have such amazing vistas and incredible mountains, we should be so proud, but sometimes, crowded together in Barcelona, we forget all about them. And they're gorgeous as anything. Eye-piercingly gorgeous. You have to come up here in the fall, when the crest line turns from one color to another, now red, now chestnut brown, now the beige of a Pyrenean cow's snout, now ochre, now orange, now deep garnet and colors you've never seen before in your life, with a sun yellow as an egg yolk. Man, I love walking through these mountains. I just love it so much. It's thrilling. The cows, the crests. And there in the distance, the Canigou. That place. Oh, how it fills the heart.

I reach the town, and the town is lovely as a postcard. With that solid, square, stately Romanesque church. The sun is already warming my shoulders, and I head farther up. The church is to my right, the first houses to my left. There are two horses, one brown and one white, fenced in, right there at the entrance to the town, just as it must have been a thousand years ago. I grab a fistful of grass and bring it up to the fence to see if I can tempt them, but they pay me no mind. Lovely. Sturdy. With valiant legs and necks like bulls. Horses of the Pyrenees, noble stock.

The butcher's shop where I buy sausage, real sausage, the good stuff, not like what they sell in Barcelona, is just a few steps from the church. When I go up into the mountains, I always stock up. The butcher's shop is so authentic. Truly frozen in time. With its old marble counters pink with all the blood. The wall tiles yellowed. And those crocheted white half curtains. The hand-lettered signs. And a fluorescent light that occasionally flickers. With big bottles of water lined up on the ground, and the shelves filled with everything you could imagine and more, all mixed together, and dusty and lined with red-and-white-checked oilcloth. Frozen in time. Behind the counter are an old man and a young girl, both with accents so strong you have to concentrate or you won't understand a thing.

But the butcher's shop is closed. I check the time. Eleven o'clock. Small towns are incredible, so chill, so relaxed in their approach to work and life. I love it. I wish everywhere was like that. I go to the bakery. Two houses down the road. Everything within spitting distance. The sunless streets are damp. The flag-stones gleam dark. The bakery's closed too. I check my watch again. Five minutes after eleven. What's the deal here. I turn and catch up with two women. Both dressed in black. Old, old women like something out of a fairy tale. White, sparse, frizzy hair. Wrinkled faces with blotches and warts, and watery lilac lips.

"Why's everything closed today?" I ask them.

One of them turns and regards me with disdain. She looks me up and down. She holds my gaze and replies, "We are in mourning."

"The butcher and the baker are in mourning too?"

The woman turns her head and doesn't answer me. Her companion, who's somewhat less of a witch, says, "Hilari from Matavaques is dead. He was killed by the Giants' son, in the forest. They were hunting and they had an accident and Hilari is dead," she says. "Hilari of Matavaques is dead. Like his father. Only twenty years old. So tragic."

I'm completely in the dark here. "A hunting accident?"

They start walking off and respond without turning. "Yes."

They leave me standing in front of the bakery. There's no note on the door. No obituary. Nothing. It's a quarter after eleven. The butcher's shop and the bakery are the only two stores in town. You can buy most anything at the butcher's, milk and juice and even pasta and rice and wine. In the bakery there's even more, it even has dish soap and scrubbers and mops.

I walk toward the bar. I figure I'll have a coffee and a croissant to stave off my hunger and bad luck. Damn, I think, the bar must be closed too. I'm shit out of luck. The bar is closed. Damn! They've got good food. Terrible coffee. That's one thing the mountains don't have, good coffee. The owners live upstairs. I ring the bell. No answer. Maybe they're at church too. I ring the bell again. The shrill sound echoes. The door to the house, right beside the bar's gates, is of red wood with frosted panes painted with stencils and pictures of vases and plants. I hear the sound of doors opening. And through the opaque white glass, I can make out a figure descending the stairs. Fantastic, I think. A very old man opens the door. Wearing espadrilles. Short white beard, droopy cheeks, a big, honking nose, and a glass eye. An ugly opaque yellow glass eye that's so poorly made it looks like plastic.

He says, "What do you want?"

I look at his glass eye. "Good morning."

He doesn't answer.

I think maybe I should have addressed his real eye. I switch. That one is like a fish eye, wet.

"Will you be opening up today at any point? I came here for a hike and I see everything's closed."

I look into his fake eye again. It protrudes more than the other one and looks like some sort of a gag. He doesn't respond.

"I was hoping for some lunch, or a coffee."

Silence.

"I thought that maybe, if you aren't going to open up today, you might sell me a baguette? Anything, just so I can make it back to my car, it's a good two hours away, down in the valley."

I address his good eye in an attempt to garner sympathy.

"No."

"Anything."

"No," he says, louder. "I need the bread for tomorrow!"

"But, sir, a baguette, it'll be stale tomorrow."

"No," he repeats. "Go away."

"Go away!" he says. And he shuts the door. He shuts the door! Right in my face. Now I'm about to get mad. Whatever happened to human kindness? Solidarity? Generosity? For the love of god. It's insane. So small-minded. I retrace my steps. He would've sold the baguette to any of the locals, he would have given it away. He treated me like a stranger, an outsider. Just like those old women did. I head back. I pass the closed butcher's shop on my way. Not even a note. Not even an obit. I've had it. I see a group of people at the end of the street, in front of the church. A lot of people. The townspeople, all in black. When I walk past, they're bringing out the coffin. The light is deep yellow. And the whole scene, the church, the old people, the dark coffin, the wreath of flowers, the two horses on the slope, the mountain backdrop, now it looks more like a postcard than ever. Lovely. If I were a painter, I would come up here and paint these kinds of paintings. Rural scenes. The old men and women, the berets, the scarves. The sunlight falling on the church, on the wooden box. The bell tower. It's so pretty I can't stay angry. It's so scenic. But, believe me, I'm still hungry, and I sure as hell don't like that old one-eyed guy's attitude, but beauty wins out. Life and death. I imagine that the hunter who was killed had long hair, like the knight Gentil. The townspeople pass me by, the coffin leading the way. Life up here is really tragic. And I stand there for a while, transfixed, just watching the scene unfold.

POETRY

I wrote this poem for a good friend of mine.

I look around at everything: the footpaths and the trees, the sky and the sun, the mornings and the nights and the stones and the stinging nettles and the cow patties and the peaks, and the rocks, and the distant smoke, and the boar paths—all of it, rhyming. I've got poetry in my blood, in my veins. I keep all my poems in my head as if inside a tidy drawer. I'm a vase filled with water. Simple, fresh water like the springs and runnels. I lie down and the verses just pour out. And I never write them down. That would kill them. Because paper is sweet river water that gets lost at sea. It's the place where all things fail. Poetry has to be free like a nightingale. Like a morning. Like the thin air at dusk. On its way to France. Or not. Or wherever it wants to go. I don't have anything to write on, anyway, and no pencil.

Poem for Jaume

Like an egg's shell, white was the sound.
Yet hair, in my face, covered me,
Like curtains, like leaves and branches,
The trees, the animal, Jaume's hands.

The light piercing, Jaume crying.
Light as air, the roe-deer running.
Don't cry, Jaume, we'll go find him,
Don't cry, Jaume, it doesn't hurt.

Like a sack of potatoes, like a child,
Like a dead buck, over your shoulder.
Don't want to make you sad, so alone, Jaume,
Don't want to leave you alone, so sad, Jaume.

After reciting my verses, I always pause for a small moment. After the words have echoed, after my voice has touched everything, and filled the spaces between all things, I am silent. To separate the poem from the rest. And I listen. The poet speaks. The poet proclaims. But the poet also listens. A bird or two. The air that once again stakes its claim as lord and master of the space between the leaves. The thin whistle the world makes, at the bottom of every ear . . .

I composed this poem for me:

Poem for Me, Hilari

I sing to the moon when it blooms full,
Round fang in the kindly night,
Expecting cat.
I sing to the frozen river,
My soul's companion,
Like a vein, like a teardrop.
I sing to the watchful wood,
Sated with fish, hares, penny buns.
I sing to the bounteous days of sun,
To the summer breeze, to the winter breeze,
To the mornings, to the evenings,
To the thin rain, to the angry rain.
I sing to the slope, the peak, the meadow,
To the stinging nettle, to the wild rosebush, to the bramble.
I sing like someone plowing a garden,
Like someone carving a table,
Like someone raising a house,
Like someone climbing a hill,
Like someone eating a walnut,
Like someone lighting a fire.
Like God creating animals and plants.
When I sing, mountains dance.

Poetry has it all. Poetry has beauty, it has purity, it has music, it has images, it has words, recited out loud. It's got freedom and the ability to move you, to let you glimpse the infinite. The great beyond. Infinity isn't on Earth and it isn't in heaven. The infinite dwells in each of us. Like a window on the top of our heads that we didn't even know was there, and that the poet's voice opens up little by little, and up there, through that crack, is the infinite.

I composed this poem for my sister, Mia. Because one day we never saw each other again:

Poem for Mia

I will be the fertilizer in your garden,
The tomato plant, the earwig,
The endive, the ornery weeds.
My heart, Mia, it is a stone.
I will dissolve slowly,
Like butter; with a hand rake,
You will comb me into the earth.
My heart, Mia, is a stone.
A smooth stone like a longing,
A small fist like love dawning.
That doesn't dampen, that doesn't break,
My heart, Mia, it is a stone.
The house, women and men, our mother,
The car, the dog, the TV, Sundays,
All of it slides like a river, over my back.
My heart, Mia, it is a stone.
I have a weight on my chest, the memory of a quarry,

Hard grief, sad poem.
Sister-bonded to your own,
My heart, Mia, it is a stone.

That last poem is one of the ones I'm most proud of. It's not a sad poem. Make no mistake. It's a melancholy poem. Because sometimes beauty leaves you gasping for air. I don't suffer much, from sadness or melancholy, but melancholy, like beauty, is important for poetry.

I learned all that on my own. The importance of melancholy to give the poem weight. And the colors of words and verses. I'm essentially a self-taught poet. An ardent enthusiast. Feeling my way through the dark. And proud of it. I don't miss the weight of tradition that burdens those who've read and studied. I shouldn't say that. In another life I read a little Verdaguer and a little Salvat-Papasseit. And that's it. From the book by Verdaguer called *Canigó*, which my mother kept in a drawer:

And higher and higher until you can see the face of the creator!

And a passage that said:

I want you,
Peasant poet.
Take this book
That celebrates our union.

In the book by Salvat-Papasseit called *Rose on the Lips*, which my mother kept in the same chest of drawers:

> Nothing is paltry and no hour is barren, nor dark is the happenstance of night!

And another passage:

> My lips are a rose
> That opens to your kiss.

They were both inscribed:

> From your Sió

And dated:

> 21 May 1964

The day my parents, Domènec and Sió, were united in holy matrimony. My mother kept poetry in a drawer. I don't remember my father. My mother told me he was a peasant poet. I asked her if we had any of his poems. My mother said he didn't write them down, he spoke them out in the open air. And then I asked her if she remembered any of his poems. And she said no.

At the time that made me angry. My mother's negligence and forgetting.

But now I think that's exactly what makes my father's poems

good, more pure, more poetic, absolutely transcendental, much better poems.

Like mine.

I wrote these two poems for my parents.

I leave space so you can breathe.

Poem for My Mother

Come here, Mama, we'll keep each other company,
Like the tiles of our house,
Like the trees at our house,
Like Jesus and Joseph and the mother of God.

Come here, Mama, we'll talk to each other
Of things that happen in the forest, at night,
Of things that happen in the heart, at night,
Of lightning that scorches the sky.

Come here, Mama, we'll sing together
Melodies that put sobbing to sleep,
Songs that make the dead dance,
Tunes that comfort, bring joy.

Inspiration—good company!—comes from distant times, and from things around us. You remember being a child, or the day you died, or all the mornings that came after, or you think of your mother, or observe the things before you, the night and the stones, and inspiration comes, and fills your cheeks and your nose with the delight of sweet wine.

I often compose my poems with someone in mind. I think about someone in my life before or in my life now and I make a poem for them. The sound of friendly applause is warm, pleasant. Palomita's little hands, the sound like walnut shells they make, like music. I like to write thinking about people because it's like a gift. Because the poet's voice conjures. Conjures up loved ones and time gone by and future time. And those named by the poet gather and join hands in a circle while the sound of his voice lasts, like a bonfire, intense and scorching hot, but that dies out, too, when the time comes.

Here's the poem for my father that I mentioned:

Poem for the Hare-Man

You sleep in the open air, like hares.
No home, no burrow, no den,
Your blanket the great outdoors,
A thicket your shelter.
Small heart full of dread,
You never shut your eyes entirely.
Hidden amongst dark shadows
You leap, you flee, you die of fright.

Like a woodworm, like a weed,
You've been invaded by wilderness.
It's gobbled up your words,
Your memories, your two children.

I never explain my poems, never.

The next one I wrote for the roe-buck who got away from us the day Jaume killed me on accident:

Poem for the Roe-Buck Who Got Away

Fly, roe-buck, run
For the hunter will come.
Through the bullet hole
Evil will get in,
Thirst will flee.

Fly, roe-buck, run
For he'll rip out your antlers,
And when you close your eyes,
He'll flay your belly
And stuff you with straw.

Fly, roe-buck, run
For far off there are greener meadows,

There are does, there is cold water,
Yellow evenings,
Fresher morns.

I like that last stanza a lot.

And in the poem for my mother, I really like the lines that say:

Come here, Mama, we'll talk to each other
Of things that happen in the forest, at night,
Of things that happen in the heart, at night.

This next poem is, without a shadow of a doubt, the poem deserving of the longest round of applause in the history of Catalan poetry:

Poem for Dolceta, Margarida, Eulàlia, and Joana

This poem is to tell you,
Women friends,
With fingers long
As orange segments:
Thanks so much
For the berries
That you gave us last night.
They were good and black and sweet
And we ate them with great delight.

Sometimes I sing out my poems. To play, to test them out. Poetry is a game, too, after all. Poets must be playful. Poetry is a serious matter, among the most serious. More serious than death and life and everything. A profound and vital matter. And precisely for that reason we poets have to know how to play and we have to know how to laugh and we have to know irony.

I composed this song for my dear Palomita. And there's so much rhythm inside the poem itself that you can't help but sing the song. I sing it in different voices, making faces, and Palomita laughs and laughs and laughs, she claps and says more, more!, and she never tires of me singing her song for her:

Poem for My Joyful Palomita

I've got myself a little dove
Who's pretty as a china doll,
One of her legs got a boo-boo
Now it ends in a wrinkled ball.

My pretty dove has seen bad things
That happened so, so far away
In the daytime she laughs and sings
But at night her fears come out to play.

She dreams of priests and soldiers,
But I tell her, don't you fear,
For, my little mourning dove,
They're all gone, away from here.

I've got myself a little dove
Cheerful as the day is long,
She calls me her sweet brother
So her brother sings this song.

EVERYBODY'S BROTHER

When the bomb fell it blew my leg right off. Zas!

Zas! No. There was blood and flesh and a smell of burned pig's hair, and the doctors had to cut off my leg.

I had always wanted a big brother. Because I just had two little brothers, like two scared little sparrows, and I would hug them and tell them not to cry.

I don't cry, because I like the forest, and the mountains, and everything in them. And I like the older brother the forest gave me. Germà, I call him, germà, brother, my sweet brother, Hilari, and since he can't hold my hand, since I need my hands to hold my crutches, he puts his palm on the back of my neck. Like a ladle.

When the bomb fell Mamá died, and Rosalía, who was our neighbor, died, too, and it cut off my leg and it cut off my brother Juan's foot. Mamá and Rosalía and Aunt Juani said the planes were coming. They were Italian planes. They told us to run and run. To the fields, to the olive groves. When we left our houses the planes arrived. We ran and ran and the bomb caught us in the football field. We ran and ran and all of a sudden Mamá shouted for us to lie facedown, "Cover your head with your hands!" We could hear the bombs falling on the rooftops. And everything was white and everything was still, and the whistling in our ears was very loud, because they'd dropped a bomb on us. They took good aim. Aunt Juani wasn't our aunt but everybody called her Auntie. When Mamá and Rosalía died in the hospital, Papá didn't say a word, and then they took us to Catalonia, first to Lérida, and then to Barcelona, and then, when Juan and I left the hospital, each with our own set of crutches, we went to La Garriga.

I like my older brother because he has the answers to so many questions, and because he knows poems. I like the forest because it's not scary. Because it's happy. Because the soldiers don't come, because there are no soldiers, and no little brothers who cry when nothing you say will get them to stop. Who moan, I want to go home, please, please, let's go home. And no sad papás. Just my older brother, Hilari, my germà, the germà of us all, of everybody who wants to be his brother or sister. Like me. I do. Even though sometimes I miss Juan and Pedro, my little crying sparrow brothers, little sparrow with a bad foot, and I wish they would come here to play in the forest, and swim in the river, and meet our other brother, and he would tell them that no more bad things are going to happen.

If you think about the war, it makes you sad. Our men wrecked all the bridges so the Nationalists couldn't come in with their war cars, and so we could escape like little ants, even the girls on crutches, and the boys on crutches. La Garriga was a really sad town. When Papá worked in the sugar factory he smelled like caramel, when he worked as a guard in La Garriga he smelled like grief.

Later we got into trucks. Headed to France. And later you couldn't travel by truck because the road was buried with stuff, with carts and baggage and even abandoned cars. I liked the mountains, they were so cold. I liked them more than everything we'd seen and more than our town and more than Barcelona and more than Lérida and more than La Garriga and more than anything. I liked the mountains because if you looked at the trees and the snow and the peaks, you could forget the war, forget crying little brothers like sparrows, and forget fear and all the rest. Snow like bleach. Clean, so clean. But you shouldn't be sad. Me, I never cry. Except sometimes when I dream. But that's not my fault. It's like when you're dreaming and you wet the bed. When I wake up from the crying dreams I curl up like a dove so my brother will sing me the song about the dove. That's me, Palomita, little dove.

We have a small home, my brother and I, like a round hole in a tooth, like a pointy tooth sticking out of a thicket of trees. We sleep in the heart of our house, which is like a den, like a bed. And when we go up on top, we can see the valley below, with all the trees holding hands like the wool of a sweater, and the sister mountains above, and the river, which you can't see, but you can hear, and sometimes we look at the moon from up there on our roof, which isn't a roof but pointy rock. Our house is so snug, I call it our little home. The four women call it the Roca de la Mort. I understand enough Catalan to know that means the

Rock of Death. One day I asked my little older brother, "Why is our house called the Roca de la Mort?"

He said, "Why are you called Eva?"

And I shrugged because nobody had ever told me. My mamá was named Elena, my papá was called Israel.

My little older brother said that nobody chooses their own name. "It's called the Roca de la Mort because people call it that. Just like you call it our little home. Things are called what people call them."

I told him, "If it's just our house, only you and me can call it our little home."

"Yes," he said, "there are names that only some people can use."

Like germà.

When we reached the coll—coll is "mountain pass" in Catalan and it is up above, far from our little patch of forest and our little home—we had to wait three days for them to open the border. I had never seen a border before. Waiting was more tiring than walking.

Later they told Papá that in the first French town they were separating children from their papás and we hid. We slept in a corral for two nights. Like hens. Like lambs. In the hay. And it smelled of manure but it was a good smell. Like food. In the corral, my sparrow brothers cried and cried because they wanted to go back home, "Please, Papá, please," they would beg. And it snowed. And later a Frenchman came who walked with just one foot, like Juan. He came to help us. And he took us to a school. To a school in a French town. But in that French school nobody studied anymore, they just slept and waited. France was a very sad country. And then Papá and I got sick and they took us to the hospital again. The cold snuck into my chest, and Papá's, like it was snowing in our hearts. And when I got better and woke up, because sometimes dying is getting better, I went back to the mountains. My papá, when he died, was so sad that he stayed in the hospital. It was a hospital for sad people. And Nono and Nona came to get Juan and Pedro, because they were orphans, and they took them back to town, just the way they wanted.

I went back to the forest alone because it was a tranquil and happy forest, on a happy mountain, for a happy little dove like me. Everything smelled really strong when I got here. And the animals buzzed really loud. All around, bzzz, bzzzz, honeybees and bumblebees and even bigger bees and flies and botflies and mosquitoes, like a party. And the grass was green and yellow, and the flowers were white and purple and blue and pink. The sky was very deep blue. The river was very cold. When we fled through this place you could barely see the river. Maybe it was scared, too, and hiding, and you could hear it only like a frightened whisper. But if you found it just once, and you saw it once, that was it. It was yours. I used to bathe in the river every day, and I still do, because the cold, cold water stabs like knives and makes the heart happy. I bathe in it every day, and every day the water is different. Sometimes the knives are bigger. Sometimes they're thinner. And I play with the leeches and the little frogs, itty-bitty, teeny-weeny, and with the tadpoles and the water striders. There was no river in my town. My town was incredibly sad. And I dry off in the sun. And sometimes the fish fly. And sometimes the four women come to bathe and bring me blueberries. Those women are funny. When they see me they go, "Psssst, pssst," like I'm a little animal. And I go, "Meowww, meowww," and they laugh: "Cheeeeep, cheep, bowww wow," and they clap and touch my hair and touch the stump of my leg. They are fun and happy, the women, but I didn't want to live with them, I want to live alone and bathe in the river every day. And fish for trout. With still, blue hands. And suddenly, bam!, got the trout. Delicious trout from the happy river. And I send little boats out into the sea! Little boats made of twigs and grass, heading down the river, leaping over rocks and rapids. And I follow them along the bank, but never into the town with the pretty bridge. In town I once asked a man with a moustache who had built the river, and he said, "God." Then I asked him who built the bridge, and he told me, "The dimoni." The dimoni is the devil. And I told him, "Wow, the dimoni makes such pretty bridges. The devil should make all the bridges in Spain. Rebuild all the bridges our men wrecked." And he looked at me with such a sad face, like he was saying, Shut up, kid, but he didn't say anything. The little boats always beat me because with the crutches I run so slow. Now I have only one shoe and one sock. I used to wear two.

I'm not the only one who returned to the forest. There are always souls passing through on the route we took to France. Every day, that same little stretch. Their belongings on their backs, their faces grim. I used to tell them they should come swim in the river, that there's no war in the mountains, that wars end but the mountains never do, that the mountains are older than war, and wiser than war, that once you're dead they can't kill you again. But they didn't want to swim. My brother calls them the Republicans. The Republicans are like me.

One day when I got to the river, my brother was bathing. It

was my first time seeing him. There are two pools in the river that are mine. One is close by, the other is far off. The first one is always in the shade. But it's deep and you can jump from the rocks and the river comes down fast and you can make little boats and move rocks to make dams. The water is always cold. On the other side there's a meadow where sometimes the roe-deer graze. There are always tadpoles in that pool, and you can reach it by going down a steep slope. It's so steep that no grass grows on it, only oaks and fir trees and stinging nettles. Or you can go the long way around, through the meadows, crossing streams and boar dens. Depends on how much of a rush you're in. I slide down the steep slope on my backside, using my crutches to push away the nettles and avoid the trees.

The second swimming hole is farther off. You have to keep walking for a long time after you pass the first pool. The second one is always sunny. And the water is calmer and there are flying fish and it's better for fishing. It's not as deep but there is more room for swimming, and the water is more still. I don't know how to swim but I'm teaching myself. You can reach the pool from the top of a hill, and there are rocks. I throw my crutches onto the rocks, and sometimes they fall into the water and then I wriggle down like a lizard. Once I fell straight into the water but it didn't hurt. I bathe naked because I'm not ashamed. And because nobody's watching me. And because the women who say, "Pssst, pssst," and the other women in the cave also bathe naked and nobody's ashamed. I wish I could've seen my mamá's thighs and breasts. My mamá was a happy mamá. The day I met my sweet Hilari, he was bathing. Belly up, with his eyes closed, his face smiling and his little willy floating. His willy was like Juan's and Pedro's, but hairy. And his skin was incredibly white and shiny like a fish's. I wasn't scared. But I had never seen a man in the river before. It was just the women and me. Maybe the men were all too sad to swim.

"Hey!" I said to him. "Hey, you!" And he stood up. "This is my pool!" Like when the older boys would take the rocks Juan and Pedro were playing with. Hey, you, dum-dum, give him back his rock. The man came out of the water and sat down on the bank. At first I didn't want to take off my clothes or get into the river; I wanted to stay like a guard dog watching over the water. But then I thought, It's my pool, I can do what I want, so I took off my clothes and jumped in. And he stood naked on one bank, with his butt and thighs all muddy. And when I turned around suddenly, I saw that he'd stuck his big toe into the river, and I told him, "You can get in if you want, but it's still my pool." He got in. And after swimming, he stayed. His name was Hilari and he didn't want to be alone. He knew a lot of things about the mountains because he has always lived here, and he knew poems, stories, and songs. I was happy living alone in the forest. I liked the forest and the occasional company of the women and the roe-deer and the rabbits. Then I found my sweet brother bathing in my pool and he came to live with me. I introduced him to the women one day, and I told him, "You have to make animal noises," and he went, "Mooooooo, moooooooooo," like a cow, and the women liked that and after that they would always wave to us from a distance and sometimes they gave us fruit, and if we caught a lot of trout, we'd give them some fish. And I showed him the other women in the cave, and he said he'd seen them before, and I told him that he shouldn't bother them and he said fine.

Today my brother wakes me up and tells me he has something to show me. "Run, Palomita, run, has de veure una cosa, you have to see this!" I grab my crutches quickly and scoot my way out of the cave. Our little home is rather high up. To get out, I grab my crutches, throw them onto the ground outside, which is always soft with grass and leaves, and then I slip down the rock like it's a slide. I'm a grasshopper with just one leg, who never gets hurt. To get into our little home, I grab my crutches and throw them inside. Clank, clank, they bang against the walls and floor. Then I grab the rocks that have bumps and ears to grab on to, and with my belly glued to the rock face, like a frog, I dangle from my hands. My arms are very strong. And then I hop with my leg and anchor it on the rock, and when I've got my bearings, I put my hands a little higher up, near the curve of the mouth of our little home, and another hop, and by then my hands are already gripping the cozy floor where we sleep, and another hop, and with my elbows on the ground, I push my belly and I'm in. I don't need anyone's help. Except when I'm really tired, then I let my brother carry me in his arms.

The early morning is fresh and the sun is warm. My brother waits in the bushes while I leave the house, and then runs in front of me and stops every once in a while so I can catch up. He turns and looks at me and then looks up at the sky and then continues on.

"Darling little Palomita," he says in a whisper, "bona companyia, such good company." When my brother puts his hand on the back of my neck, it's like he's holding out his hand for me to walk with him. Sometimes, with his hand on my nape, he recites poetry. Or he tells me things about the pica-soques, the nuthatches. "Pica-soques, pica-soques, pica-soques pica bé," he sings. Hilari is my older brother, but he's an itty-bitty older brother who says, "Palomita, look. Palomita, come. Palomita, you have to see this. Palomita, will you keep me company?"

Now he says, "Palomita, you can't make any noise."

I can be very, very quiet. My crutches grip the ground in silence, like bird legs.

"We're getting close," he whispers.

We walk through the trees and the bushes, along the slope, beneath the branches. And he says, "Sssssh, ssssh, veus? You see it?"

I can't see a thing.

"Over there," he says. "Over there."

I see brown leaves, and yellow leaves, and green leaves, and gray and brown and green trunks, and there it is, I see it now! For the first time ever. A man like a dog. Like a crazy man who lived in my town, who would call women whores and bitches. With long, dirty hair and twisted fingernails. He is skinny and crouching and naked and we can see his whole backside. It's dirty. His head is on the ground. We get a little closer. He's eating grass. And then he sticks his face into the black earth and eats dirt. Grass with dirt. Roots. Worms.

"That man is my father," says my sweet brother.

My father was called Israel. My mamá, Elena.

"What's your father's name?" I ask.

"Domènec," he answers.

And I don't bring up the fact that his papá is eating dirt, because he can see that for himself.

III

CRUNCH

Don't come looking for me. Blind as I am. Immense as they made me. Deaf, from my ear-shattering birth. You have no need for my voice nor for my perspective. Leave me be.

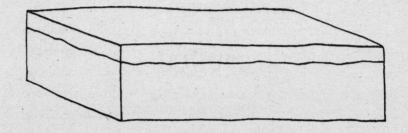

My slumber is so deep that it slips beneath the seas. The sea used to cover me, millennia ago, I can scarcely recall. Blind and deaf and sleeping as I am. Out, out. Grow, mosses. Reproduce, wee beasties, the pitter-patter of your tiny feet rocks me to sleep, the creeping of your roots consoles me. Nothing lasts very long. Not a thing. Not stillness. Nor calamity. Nor the sea. Nor your ugly little children. Nor the earth that tolerates your puny little feet.

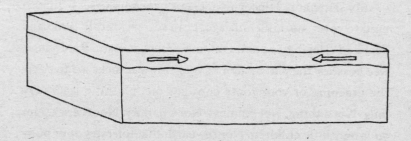

Oh, to think of that woeful crunch, the impact.

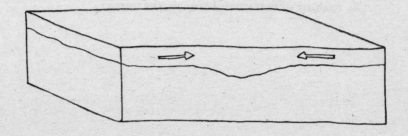

The terrible awakening.

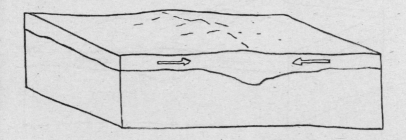

If I made the effort to evoke the deafening crunch. The incandescent, red, uncontrollable depth. If I recollect the slow, terrible crash, the annihilating blind violence, the jerking and the earthquakes, the columns of smoke and dust, the tearing deep into the hot liquid rock.

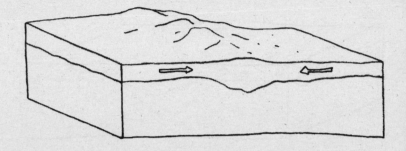

If I thought about how we hurled your little tiny feet. How we tore out your roots, clinging miserably to clumps of earth. How we destroyed your house, how it was never the same again. If I thought back to how you died. How all of you died, you who didn't fly, you who didn't run, you who were too fat, too heavy, too dumb, too weak.

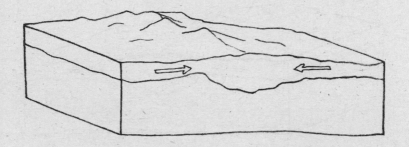

How you all died, while we took off. Up, up into the air. Tons upon tons of rock and earth, granite, gneiss, and calcite. Up to the heavens we rose from the depths. With all the tenacity, all the patience, the slowness, the destruction. The dark surge lifted us into the air, the brute strength sent us up, the rock coiled, the earth piled upon itself, heaped up, folded, burst.

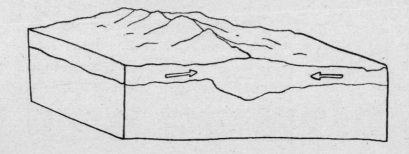

Now leave me be, let me sleep in peace, rootless broods, rambling weeds, piddling storms, sad trees. More of you came, more always come. To make nests and to make dens and to stomp your hooves. To make green shoots grow from split trees. And my rock faces and my peaks and my crests were new lairs for you, my poor, miserable wretches.

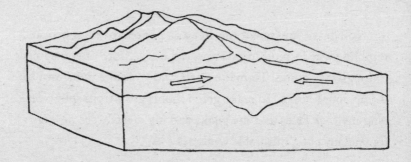

Come here, come, I shall give you a stretch of my back so you can build a house there.

But don't make me speak another word. Silence. Enough.

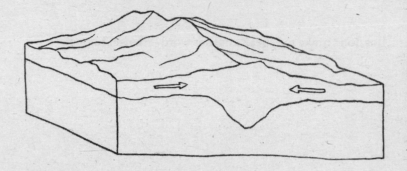

Don't make me tell you what will happen then, once you have all sunk your roots deep down into me, when your burrow is nice and comfy, loyal, and good to you, when you've guzzled my fresh water, when you've closed your little eyes, and you've named your offspring. Then a boom of blind violence will thunder down, much older than I, much more infinite than I, much less merciful than I. And it will exert new forces.

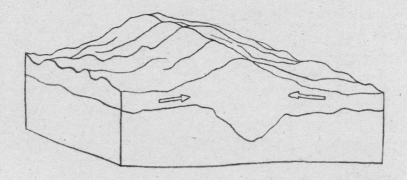

The continents will curl up over their foundations. The rock walls will grind with the blows, the sky will suddenly darken, the rivers of lava will flow, setting everything aflame, the sea will make way, and everything will shake as the volcanoes erupt and the air fills with smoke and ash. The mountains we'd been, the houses and the dens and the lairs and the terraces and the crests we had been, shall cease to be. And our peaks will become valleys and plains, and our ruins, our remains, will become tons of rubble sinking into the sea, new mountains.

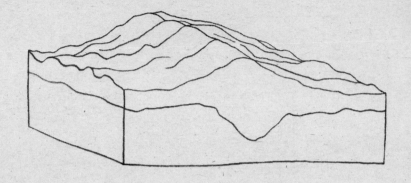

The movement will have begun again. The disaster. The next beginning. The nth end. And you will all die. Because nothing lasts long. And no one remembers the names of your children.

BIRTHING BABIES

All their stories are lies. Listen to me. All the stories they tell. The ones that say we are evil. Lies. The ones that say we are good and beautiful as silver and that all the men become mesmerized and throw themselves into the pools. Lies. Those that say we are a mysterious mystery, lies. Most men are liars. The men who invent stories and those who tell them. The ones who cut us out, who collect us and force us inside words, so we are the story they want to tell, with the moral they want to explain. Cut out and shrunk down to fit into their little tiny heads. Tiny and dumb, but not any less evil.

Blanca, your mother, waddled like a goose and went here and there, belly growing ever bigger. Her abdomen was full and hard like a drum, and her breasts had swelled and would soon have milk. Like magic. Like true magic, because a whole baby would come out of her vulva, with all its finger- and toenails, and little eyes and tongue, and that baby would be you. A pretty little crybaby, because in every mother's eyes her baby is pretty, but you were truly pretty.

Blanca, your mother, wanted company. Before. And she went to find a man. And she found one. She found a strong man who worked the fields, with such big hands at the ready, who had skin dark as night and black-and-yellow eyes because he'd seen sad things and lived far from the country where he'd been born. And they loved each other in the evenings, Blanca and your father, always beneath the trees and atop the grass. Blanca would put her hands on his chest, and he would say, in another tongue, "Look, like a butterfly." But Blanca didn't want to save any man, after so many years of wanting to save men. She didn't want to bring him home. She wanted only his seed, to bear a girl, brown as a chestnut. Filled with laughter and ideas. Truly lovely, because she was made of meat. Yummy, juicy meat! Not all white and silvery like a lily. No. She was made of real flesh. The kind you can sink your teeth into! Grrrarr.

Lots of animals give birth at night. The mares won't if you're looking at them, to protect the filly from your eyes and your intentions. But Blanca went into labor in the morning. One spring morning that dawned cold. You remained still, inside her, ready, and her whole belly squirmed in a shuddering spasm. "The baby's coming," she said. And we sat her down in the back of the cave, on the blankets and sheets, and she couldn't get cool. And then out came the brown plug, and water and water and water from inside her, as if her vulva were a spring. And you, you couldn't swim anymore, you were almost here, and Alba and Flora ran off to find the women who know about birthing babies.

I stay with Blanca, and I tell her to breathe with the contractions, and I hold her hands when she can stand to be touched. And I give her an infusion of thyme. And I put more water on to boil and I prepare more blankets, and Blanca moans on and off, and then, her head all fuzzy, she says, "I'm fine, I'm happy, I am. Now we'll have a little baby to play with."

The sun reaches its midmorning height and Blanca is crawling. And she squats and breathes heavy and moves her hips from side to side, and she says, "It hurts more and more, coming faster now," and I tell her, "Breathe, breathe, Blanca," and I remember the other times. The times I carried babies inside me. Three, like three stars. And I tell her, "Don't you remember, Blanca, don't you remember the last time you had a baby in your womb?" And Blanca says, "You forget the pain so fast . . ." And she smiles a little and then she goes, "Aiiish . . ." and lays her palms flat on the ground.

"My little ones had hair like wet hay," I tell her. "And the man who's nameless now because I erased him when he raised a hand to me and said, 'What was I thinking, marrying a water sprite!' and then he brought it down, hard, against my head and my cheeks and my chest. That man said that children belong to their fathers, not their mothers. And I said no. I said I'd carried them inside me all that time, and they were made of me, and they'd come out of me, they'd cracked me open like an egg that could never be closed again. And he shouted, 'Shut up, shut up, you just shut up, you whore, you stupid vessel.' I told him my children would be like birds and they wouldn't love him. He threatened me, saying that if I ever came back, he would kill all three of them. But my children grew and like birds they flew from him. This baby will be ours," I tell her.

And then Alba and Flora arrived with a woman who knew about birthing babies. There are always four of those women. And they all have white hair. There's the one in charge, her name's Joana and she wears her long hair messy, and her face is severe and she doesn't speak, but her eyes are full of the things she knows. There's the one who's always laughing, she's named Dolceta and she wears her hair in braids, and she's Blanca's friend because they both like to joke and laugh. Then there's Margarida, who's always crying. And Eulàlia, who tells us stories. She tells us stories we love because they're never in the voice or through the eyes of those men who write the bad stories.

The women who know how to birth babies live in the forest, but I've never been to the cave where they sleep. Eulàlia told me one day that it wasn't like our cave, that it was a bandits' cave. But maybe that was a riddle.

The woman they bring today has short white hair, and wears a purple robe with a sash. Alba leads her, and Flora brings up the rear, and the woman follows them, nimble and calm as a rabbit.

Her face is candid and attentive. She enters the cave and Blanca opens her arms as if she were a little girl who wanted to be picked up.

"Here she is, this is her," says Alba, and the woman approaches Blanca, takes her by the hands, and says, in a whisper, "We're animals and we know how to give birth. It comes naturally to us. People are animals, too, and sometimes we forget that. Just listen to the baby and listen to the pain. Hold tight to the rock," she tells her. "Breathe," she tells her.

And Blanca turns herself over to the woman as if she were a mother. Then Blanca takes off her clothes.

"That's it, that's it," says the woman. "Naked, like the animals. What's your name, little beastie?" she asks.

And Blanca says her name. "Where did you learn about birthing babies?" she asks her, moaning.

"Helping cows give birth," says the woman. "And I had two children," she says. "The first one like a stubborn stalk, wouldn't come, wouldn't come out. Second one like a frog, hopped right out on his own."

She feels Blanca's belly.

"It's coming face-first," she says. "Calves lead with their legs."

Blanca doesn't scream, she stops breathing, grips the wall, and moans from deep inside, a long, painful moan, her face sopping wet and her hair stuck to her head and her hands all white from clenching the stone face.

The woman touches her and looks at her and says, "You are wide open and soon we'll see the little head." Blanca gets on all fours and breathes. The woman tells us, "Bring more rags and more water." And we bring more rags and more water, and Blanca moans and grinds her teeth harder and harder and then all of a sudden she lets out a groan that starts with an aaaaah, an aaaaah deep inside, an aaaaah that's soft and coarse and hurts to hear.

"Squat, hunker down, feet on the ground, like you are taking a shit," says the woman, and Blanca lifts her knees and places her feet flat against the floor and then the woman adds, "It's coming fast, I can already see the little head."

"I'm scared," says Blanca. And the woman says, "Don't be scared," and she says it confidently and severely and Blanca pushes. The woman kneels behind Blanca and stays there, with both hands beneath her womb. One arm in front, the other arm behind Blanca's ass, round, white, and full. The woman has her hands at the font where life emerges, as if harvesting grapes, as if gathering handfuls of water, and then the little head comes out all at once. "Breathe, breathe," she says, "now come the shoulders." And she puts her hands around the baby's neck, like a fish, still wrapped, all purple, and out come the shoulders. The woman supports its little back with her forearm, and its little butt—which comes out fast—with the other hand, and out come the legs, little and curled up, so perfectly formed. Blanca puts her hands back down on the ground, like a cow, and you are completely out now, and you take in air and you cry a big cry, and Blanca puts her hips down on the rock, on the blood and the blankets, with the dark, thick cord between her legs. You're a girl! The woman places you on your mother's swollen belly, between her breasts like two mountains. Your eyes are wrinkled and your hands are wrinkled and your hair is dark, and Blanca smiles a lot, with a laugh so very bright, and eyes so very bright, and skin so very bright, and with a girl like a dark butterfly at her breast. And then comes the placenta.

After you'd been born, Blanca, all foggy and tired, asks the woman, "What's your name?" And she replies that her name is Sió, and that she's very, very sleepy. She curls up in a corner and falls fast asleep. And she sleeps an entire day. She sleeps deeply and when she wakes we give her thyme soup and then she goes back to her home.

Three days later, when you are nursing like a little calf and Blanca waddles around like a plucked goose, she tells me: "Her hands were warm."

And I don't know what to say and she continues: "Her hands were warm like the folks in the towns, that woman who birthed the little calf." (She named you Bruna but we all called you the little calf.) "She wasn't hanged, that woman. She has a house with windows and lives in the towns."

I put down the sock I'm knitting. Little booties for little footsies.

"Blanca, what makes you say that, now?"

You are glued to her breast, suckling and suckling, and Blanca looks at you as if in a dream and says to me: "She won't come back. She was lost, she'd gotten lost. Alba helped her find her way home."

I shake my head because I don't like that, and we sleep the sleep of the restless for a few nights because you cry so much, and because we imagine them, the folks in the towns, coming, cornering us.

THE SNOW

I get out of the car and the dog greets me and I knock on the
door and ask to come in and once I'm sitting at the kitchen table
I blurt out: "I tried to tell your mother and she didn't like it. But
now that Sió's dead, I'll say it to you, Mia. You've got somebody
in this house."

She looks at me calmly. "Is it somebody dead?"

"What's left of 'em," I say.

"With bad intentions?"

"Better out of the house than in."

"Like all animals," she says. "Is it my father?"

"I don't know."

"Is it blind?"

"I don't know."

"Is it Hilari?"

I don't know if it's Hilari.

"Can I think about it?" she asks.

I don't go into Matavaques if I can help it. I avoid looking at its windows. I look at the garden and the vegetable patch and the ridge on the other side. When I sense it, I imagine a man. But it isn't a man. I imagine a man so I'll feel a little less afraid. An angry man. Violent and out of control, with the dark certainty of strength. Pouting, like a child. Hidden in a corner. Steeped in the poison of his own failure. Incubating rage and waiting like a brooding hen whose eggs have been stolen.

It used to really snow. It snowed so much that it rose up like prison walls along the roadsides. Like labyrinths. Like castles. Kids would grab sacks and slide down the slopes without sleds. Their butts on the sacks, on the snow. You would hear them laughing and shouting over the absolute silence of the mountains after a snowfall. As if everything, trees and beasts, had been struck dumb by shock. By the blinding whiteness. Snow like a white hand covering their mouths. Kids celebrating. Because you can't control snow, sort of like death. It comes when it wants to and changes everything. The weatherman Tomàs Molina says it will snow. Today. I say it won't. I can tell when it's about to snow, because the light is white. When it's about to rain the light is gray, silvery. You start to see the gray light and the white light almost a day before. Depending on their intensity, you know how soon it will rain or snow.

My grandmother used to seek out water with iron rods, like two Ls, and her father knew when it was going to rain, and people—who were generally not fond of my great-grandfather because they said he was scary—would come to see him and ask him when to plant their crops. One day when we were gathering brushwood with my grandmother, I asked her what the cascades were. I had always seen them, the cascades, hanging in the middle of the sky, like the clouds. Some of them thicker, some of them skinnier, of a transparent, lovely, muffled blue like the river. My grandmother looked up at the patch of sky I was pointing to and exclaimed: "Oh, dear lord, my girl. What've we done to you." And she said no more. My grandmother was named Dolors. Nana Dolors didn't say that beneath the cascades there are wells and underground rivers. She didn't say that the cascades signal water, and that only she, me, and my great-grandpa could see them. That was how she found water. And she didn't say that those who see cascades see other stuff. But not with their eyes. With their bellies. With each and every one of the hairs on their arms and on the napes of their necks, and with their livers and their lungs and their hearts and their bile and in all the parts of the body that feel fear and grief. And she didn't say a word about the darkness in the corners. Not a word about the things that are so sad they're like a slap in the face. Not a word about the things you must never do under any circumstances. Or about the ones that die and don't leave. Or about the holes where the earth breathes. Or about the balance.

Sometimes my husband jokingly calls me the Snow Queen. Because my name is Neus, which means "snow." And I always know when it's going to snow. I call my husband Agustí, which is the name his mother gave him, but everybody else calls him the Bailiff. Except for our daughters, who call him Papa. In the story of the Snow Queen, she had a mirror. A mirror that, when you looked into it, would reflect back only sad and bad things. Once some trolls were carrying the mirror to the Winter Palace and it slipped away from them and fell and shattered into a thousand pieces. And those thousand pieces scattered everywhere. They got into some people's eyes, and then everything those people saw was sad and ugly. And they got into some people's hearts, and they could feel only bitterness and grief. And a shard of the mirror got stuck in one of my eyes, and I see some sadnesses, I see where a person's been hurt, and I sense the dead who are stuck in this world. And if I have the strength, if I have the energy, or if they get too close to people I care about, I tell them to go.

The telephone rings. It's Mia. "Neus," she says, "get it out of the house." I tell her I can come over tomorrow. On Mondays Mia and my daughter Cristina go out walking. "Let's do it during the day," I say. She says she can make lunch for me, I say there's no need. "I'll come at ten. You'll have to wait outside." And I think about Tomàs Molina saying it'll snow.

The next day the sky is like the belly of a table, low and flat and gray. When Domènec died and Sió was left alone, I would visit her every week. I wasn't even married at the time. I would bring her green beans, or zucchini, or anything that provided an excuse to pay her a visit. And years later, when Sió lost her marbles, I came by often too. But not often enough. It's never enough. If I did have to go into the house, I would keep to the kitchen. The kitchen is a good kitchen. Or if I could, I'd keep to the threshing floor, out front, where the sun beat down hard and hot. Our patch of mountain has its own microclimate.

When I get to Matavaques, Mia comes out with her dog.

"Do you need anything?" she asks me.

I don't need anything.

I go in. The house waits for me in silence. Surprised. Expectant. It is an old house but not very large, for tenant farmers or shepherds. The entrance sits over three steps like three teeth. It's a small entrance, with rough walls and unmatched floor tiles. The coatrack and the shoe rack. A streaky wooden built-in closet. A solid table with a tray of keys and papers and letters. The kitchen is to the left, with white tiles that occasionally sprout a blue flower. The sink is of pink marble, there's a window with embroidered curtains and an old rack shelf that displays the dishes, all white. A sturdy table, dark and polished and gleaming from years of use, and a bench that must be quite old, with linen cushions, and a vase with dried flowers, and small chairs and a television. Mia is good about maintaining her furniture. Saving unsavable things. And the house is neat and welcoming. Not like our house, always messy. Everything all over, that man of mine and those grandkids of mine.

The stovetop area is new. With a vent made of wood, but you can tell this is wood that's never lived in a forest, that was cut and polished by soulless machines. The fireplace is lit. It's an old hearth. Built into the floor of the house, set into the walls. White, edged in wood, and a tiled chimney black with soot. A good kitchen. There's a separate walk-in pantry with doors, I've never been inside. To the right of the entryway is the room where Mia sleeps, which, if I'm not mistaken, was Grandpa Ton's. I go in there to nose around, because I know nothing's in there. It's pretty. Yellow walls. Two tall windows. A hope chest and a dresser and a wardrobe, big and solid, with a simple border carved into the wood. A small mirror with a porcelain basin. A chair covered in clothes clean enough to wear again. A bedside table with more dried flowers and Vicks VapoRub and medicines and a small lamp and a white radio and a photo of Mia and

Hilari from when they probably weren't even twenty years old. And books. Toni Morrison. Marta Rojals. Stieg Larsson. With the Bookmobile library bus sticker. She has a little brown mat beside the bed, which must be where Lluna sleeps. Her bed has a headboard and feet of dark wood. It's a warm bedroom.

Nana Dolors's father, my great-grandfather, would sometimes take someone aside and tell them: "Say goodbye because you're going to die." That was why people were afraid of him. Because a few days later, whoever it was he had singled out really would die. And when they saw my great-grandfather coming, people started to tremble. The man didn't have an easy time of it. He had a murder of crows circling over his head. You can't go around saying things like that. Not even if you see them. Not even if you know them. Not even if you know them with the same certainty you know that the sun will come up in the east. That's what my grandmother would tell me. Ssssh and buttoned lips. Buttoned so tightly that she never explained anything to me, not what she saw or what she did or how she did it. There was only one thing my grandmother would tell me. "The dead are dead. Don't touch them, my girl, and don't talk to them."

It's time. The problem is upstairs. I go over to the wood staircase with coffee bean tiles. It's upstairs and already waiting for me. Expectant and unhappy. Gooseflesh rises at my tailbone, then spreads up my whole back. I begin slowly. Calm. As I go up the steps. Like a mother. Like a grandmother. Sometimes these things have never had a mother or a grandmother. I nicely tell it that it has to leave. I tell it that this isn't its house. This isn't its house anymore. It's okay. I explain why this is no place for it anymore. "You no longer belong here," I tell it. "You have to go.

You have to find the path." Its grief and rage weigh heavy in my stomach. In my liver. It approaches and clings to me and sticks into me like a thick, rusty hook. It gets mad. It gets really mad. Full of rage. Full of black juice. All my hairs stand on end, like quills, like needles. And then it starts. Bastard. It doesn't speak. They don't speak. They don't speak in any way I can understand. They have no words they can use. They only have all that pain, all that hatred, all that dirty water.

I don't lose my temper. I again insist that it must leave. You can't lose your temper with these things. You can't fly off the handle. It's terrible if you do. When you fly off the handle, bad things happen. They win. They cause harm. So. "This is not your house. This is not your house. It's not your house anymore. Out. Begone. Find the path. This is no longer your place, this is no place for you, not anymore."

Sometimes you can get rid of them, these things. Some of them are people. Others, I don't know what they are. Some things can't be understood. I don't know where they go when they leave. I don't know if there's something beyond. I don't know anything. But you can get rid of some of them. You can comfort them like a baby. You can calm them down. You can explain to them what must be explained to them. And after hours, once they are small and docile and calm, they leave.

Some you can't get rid of. There are really big things in this world. Really bad things, and all you can do is battle night and day to get them to leave, to curl up and hide elsewhere. So they come out of where they're stuck and rotting, and go do it some other place.

I go into the bedroom at the top of the stairs. It's a master bedroom. Worn wooden floor. Large, old, tall bed with a gilded headboard painted with a Virgin Mary, and a chubby baby Jesus, who's already a toddler, and a sheep, and a Saint Joseph. I think this must be Sió's bedroom. And before that, it would have been Sió and Domènec's bedroom. Mia doesn't use it now. It smells of bags of herbs for the linens and of the liquid used to kill woodworms.

I stretch out on the bed, which is hard and has a yellowed white bedspread. I put my hands on my belly and close my eyes. It squirms inside me like a snake. Nasty thing. But I tell it what I have to say. Without losing control. Severe. Deathly afraid. I talk and talk and talk and repeat the same things over and over. "Out. Out. Leave. Leave."

But when I open my eyes, it's before me. Horrifying. Completely dark and with two immense, elongated white eyes. I don't move. Its face draws close to me, it's not a face at all. Mouth like a hole. I would scream but the scream is stuck in me like a bone swallowed down the wrong pipe. It'd do me no good to scream. It's not here, I tell myself. It's not here. And it looks at me impassively. It's not here. It's a child yawning with that mouth. A sleepy child with those eyes. A monster. With that gaze, terrible as all the pain in the world. Those frenzied eyes. "Out. Out. Leave. Out. This is not your house. This is not your house. This is not your house. Out. Out. Out."

And then it leaves.

I get off the bed. My feet feel so heavy, and my legs and my knees. Getting old, Neus. I go to the door and I lean on the frame. I look back at the bed. I look in the stair closet, but it's not there. It's not in the bathroom either. I go downstairs. Nothing in the kitchen. Nothing in the entryway. Nothing in the bedroom. I concentrate and listen. It's not there.

I pull myself together in the entryway and I go out.

"Would you like a coffee or something?" asks Mia.

It's drizzling.

"No," I say, "I'm tired, I'm going home."

"Thank you," she says.

"Did the dog go upstairs?" I ask.

"Not much."

"Do you want me to tell you where it was?"

"No," she answers without hesitating.

I nod. Some of those things like stairs.

"Goodbye, Mia."

When Sió lost her marbles, my husband said that sometimes, to survive, you have to throw dirt on the memories, but those who've suffered too much always throw on too much dirt. Agustí thinks a lot about our town history. He searches for the why behind things. Analyzes it. That's his way of finding peace. Understanding things, people. But not everything can be understood, my dear.

I get into the car. Drops small as needles fall onto the glass. That's not snow, Tomàs Molina. I wave goodbye to Mia, she goes into the house, and I drive off. I grip the steering wheel hard and shift into second and the seat is soft and comfy. It smells like that pine air freshener Agustí buys. The road isn't paved, and the car bounces. The mountain slope is to my left. There's a guy walking in the middle of the road, with dark hair and a cane. I slow down. Who takes a walk on this road in this weather? I think. Who is he? He's going to see Mia. He's young. And then we cross paths.

But as I pass him, I turn my face away from him, downward, toward the mountain and the river. I turn it abruptly, quick as a flash, and I'm sorry not to say hi, but I just can't. I'm tired. I don't want to see them, all the shadows and all the sad things clinging to his jacket.

FEAR

"I could be your mother," she says. And another day she'll say, "I'm not your mother." Separated by all the things that happen in between. And inside me all the things that don't make sense somehow do, and all the things that should make sense no longer do. Because if she'd had me at nineteen, or eighteen, I don't know, but I suppose I can imagine it, she could be my mother. But she never will be my mother, not even if she wanted to and I wanted her to, but I don't want that and neither does she. Sometimes I'm just as I once was. Other times it's like the person I used to be never existed, as if he'd slipped out through the hole in my head, and the only thing left is black fear, and the things heavy around my neck. And I can't stop looking at the darkness of my one eye that can no longer see and getting upset, and thinking I'll never be who I was, and that they didn't kill me but they did ruin me for the rest of my days. And thinking that someday I'll have to die again, and it's so scary, dying.

I should have died then so I wouldn't have to face it again. Then I wouldn't have learned fear. Because there are things you don't ever want to learn, that you shouldn't ever learn, and you end up learning them forever. And you can't *do* anything, you can't *want* anything, you can't *feel* anything, not with all that fear. You can't go back to being who you once were, before you learned fear. Once fear gets you, that's it, it's over. And then you have to take the pills, and try to sleep, and you have to do it again the next day, and the one after that.

When people come up to visit us I tell them this is our retreat, a country house for inspiration, to write novels, that sort of thing. And my friends laugh. My friends who are patient, that is, because most people get tired real quick of waiting for you to be okay.

Anyway, I wanted to talk about all the good things up here and how the mountains and the fresh air do a body good, especially if the top of your head's been blown off.

Once upon a time Clara and I slept together, spooning in a bed. Once upon a time two burglars entered our home. And one had a gun and he forced us out of bed and made us kneel on the rug. He pointed the gun at my head and I lowered my head like a little dog, and Clara screamed and the man screamed over her screams, wanting to scare us, but we were already scared, and with all that screaming and all that waving of the gun over my head, it went off, and the bullet entered and exited my skull, and the men ran off and Clara jumped out the window, which wasn't that far from the ground, to find help, and I stayed on the rug, because the beeping that came after the shot was incredibly loud inside my brain, and because I couldn't move, the idea of moving didn't even spark inside me.

But that wasn't what I wanted to think about. I wanted to think about when I got out of the car and thought how pretty the house looked, halfway up the crest, so hidden you couldn't even hear the cars on the road, like something out of the fairy tales my mom would tell me when I was a little boy. It was my mom who decided we would go up into the mountains, and who found Can Grill, and who packed for both of us and put me in the car and before long we were there. Because of the noise that came in through the windows of our apartment in Barcelona, what with the cars and all the buildings and the pointy corners and the straight lines and the shouting and the laughing, I felt so hemmed in that I didn't want to go outside. My anxiety expanded like a sponge when I stepped out onto the sidewalk, which felt gray and sunken and vulnerable beside the buildings. And my mother said, "Enough is enough," and she said that if we went someplace where there were only trees, I'd have to leave the house at some point.

When I woke up they said it was a miracle. And everyone stood at the foot of the bed and there were so many questions and my mother bought the newspaper and showed me my photos. And then, when they all left, I cried because I was so incredibly tired of seeing them, of repeating the same few answers over and over. The bullet had robbed me of my vision in one eye, and had given me a slight limp in my left leg, sometimes it doesn't even feel like my leg anymore. And that was that. The doctors said I was lucky. My love escaped through that hole too. Maybe if

I had loved Clara more, they would have shot me in the head and I would have woken up and loved her even more. But when I woke up I didn't want to love her anymore. Clara was crying at the foot of the bed when I told her I no longer loved her and then, when my mother came back from the hospital cafeteria, she left. I know that my mom still calls her sometimes. And I wish her well, but I don't want to have to take care of her. And by that I don't mean protect her from home invasions. I mean worry about her, I mean ask her how her day went, I mean think about her and think about the things we'll do together. Now I just want to be alone. That's why I liked the house, because it's out in the middle of nowhere. You can't see anything else. We face the valley, and on the crest in front of us there's only forest and pasture. The river passes beneath our feet, and if you're quiet, you can hear it. The house has a sundial on the facade that I don't know how to read, apparently there are some calculations you have to make. And it has a useless little balcony. And two floors. And a kitchen made entirely of wood with a ceiling so low your hair brushes the beams. It has a little pantry and small windows so the cold doesn't get in and a fireplace, built with silvery gray rock, which I always light because the fire is pretty to look at. And upstairs there's the bathroom and the floors are all wood, they creak and moan when you walk on them and even when you don't, and the pink and red sofas and armchairs and red carpets. The wood is constantly moaning and expanding and shrinking; I think if any intruders burst in here, we'd hear them before they found the bedrooms. Upstairs there's also the bathtub and toilet, in separate rooms, and the bedroom where my mom sleeps and the bedroom where I sleep, and in the room with the armchairs there's another fireplace, which I hardly ever light so I don't have to keep an eye on two fires.

We walk every day, my mom and I. From the house we take the path with the tall grasses and then we veer downhill, and we follow cattle trails, and sometimes people trails, downhill, in a zigzag that brings you to the river's edge.

Sometimes we have to push aside brambles and branches and nettles, and there's an electric fence for the cattle I have to open and then close back up. The path is covered in piles of shit. The river is called Ritort, a pretty name, and it's incredibly cold, and rushes by fast, and I imagine it as a tongue licking all the stones clean. My mother doesn't like me to throw stones into the river, but when I go there on my own I spend a long time skipping stones, and my record is five skips, which is pretty good.

If you go uphill instead, you reach our nearest neighbors. A house called Matavaques—cattle slayer—and no, I didn't make up that name. There must be some story behind it, but I can't tell you what it is. Anyway, I was the one who said, "Let's give this path a try." A path that ambled upward, like the cows. You had to hold on to the trees a little, it was that steep. "Oriol!" my mom called out to me, worried I wouldn't make it with my bum leg, but I felt I could and I was bored of always going down toward the river. And when we got up there, we saw that we were behind a house, in the garden. We would have to jump over a fence and I said, "Let's leave," and my mom said, "No, come on, now that we've come up here we should say hi." And I said, "But, Mom, this is the back way and we might frighten them." And my mom said, "Nah, it's okay." My mom is always saying that, and then just doing whatever she feels like doing. I said, "You can't just walk into somebody's house through the back door!" And she said, "Well, then you stay here." Then you stay here! she said. And she jumped over the fence, and then she helped me over. The same woman who had worriedly called my name as we started down the path. We walked around the vegetable patch, and I could make out onions and endives and lettuce and that was it. And coming up through the vegetables was some thick, strong, ugly sort of grass that spread toward the corner of the house like it had a will of its own. And then a dog appeared. It was a big dog with long white fur and two black spots, one across its back like a saddle, and another on its face, on one eye, like a pirate. He bounded over fast once he saw us, barking like a lunatic, barking and barking right in our faces, and kept his back flat and his eyes on us so we wouldn't come closer. I crouched a little bit, super slowly, and laid my cane on the ground. And then the woman appeared and shouted, "Lluna, shhhhhtt," and the dog barked twice more and then was quiet. The woman came over without a word, and just looked at the two strangers coming out of her vegetable patch. Then I said hello, and I apologized, and my mother explained that we were renting out Can Grill and the woman went, "Ah," and patted the dog's back. And they talked for a little while about the mountains, the town, my mom's impressions of it all, and the woman said she was the butcher and my mom said, "We'll be in to buy some meat, of course," and as they talked, I looked at the woman. She had such shiny eyes. Such pretty eyes. They made you want them to look at you and for her to tell you things, because she wasn't smiling but her eyes were gleaming like she was smiling on the inside. And then the rest of her face was coarse, rough-hewn; it wasn't that she wasn't pretty, it was just that her features were those of a large mammal, like a horse or a cow, but her eyes were incredibly lovely, and maybe her face not being as lovely as her eyes made her eyes even lovelier, and the fact that she wasn't good-looking and didn't smile and spoke slowly made you want her to tell you more things still. She was younger than my mom, she must have been fifty years old, maybe more, maybe less. She wore a blue short-sleeved shirt and her round arms were covered in freckles. Her hair was the exact same color as her eyes. I stared at them the whole time and it almost scared me, when her eyes looked at me. Then she extended a hand to us and said her name was Mia, and the dog walked through our legs and she said, "Go ahead, let her sniff you, that way she'll get to know you." Then she asked if we wanted coffee and my mom said, "No, thanks so much, maybe another day." And she said, "Okay, another day." And my mother again said that we would come by the butcher shop, and she asked, pointing to the hens, if she sold eggs, too, and Mia said yes but that they weren't from her hens. Then we left, down along the road out front, because we didn't dare go through her vegetable patch again. As we went down the path, which was longer and easier going than the more direct route, up the mountain, my mom said she liked that neighbor and I said I did too.

And we went to her butcher shop. It turned out she also sold milk and cheese and nuts and dried fruits and biscuits and pasta and we bought a ton of stuff. The shop smelled wonderfully of raw meat, of chicken patties and pork sausages, delicate and delicious. And my mom said, "Half a kilo of ground beef and a few pork ribs, to throw in the stew," and blah, blah, blah. And I was so embarrassed. Like I didn't want to be there, thirty-three years old and buying ground beef with my mother. And I sort of liked that feeling of embarrassment. I stood off to one side and looked at the street through the glass and then my mother bought the eggs that weren't from Mia's hens, and I definitely did like that embarrassment, hot and coiled up inside me, it had been so long since I'd felt it, it'd been so long since I'd felt anything.

That was why I went up to see her later, up the longer road. Alone. First I thought about leaving my cane behind but then I was scared of falling. I didn't tell my mother I was going to see her, I said I wanted to go for a walk, after the walk we'd already taken that day together. And I went up to the house, slowly, because the weather was nice, and because the road was long and I didn't want to get too tired and I didn't want to sweat. When I got there, I saw the sign that said Matavaques, which I hadn't noticed that first day, and I liked the name of that house. Apt for a butcher. And then the dog appeared, and came running over to me, barking, and I thought about laying my cane on the ground, but then I said, "Lluna," and she wagged her tail and barked a little less, but without looking at me, and she went behind me, which meant she was giving me permission to enter the property. When I got to the door, I thought maybe she wouldn't be there, and I thought maybe I should leave her a note, or maybe it would be weird to leave a note, and then I knocked, using my fist because there was no doorbell. When she opened up she didn't seem surprised or particularly welcoming, but she smiled a little, this time, or maybe it was just her eyes shining, like they were made of glass, and I wanted to say something I'd been thinking about the whole way up, but all I said was "Hello."

And she went: "Good afternoon."

And since I didn't say anything more, she added: "Would you like to come in?"

And I went in and the dog came in with us.

Now, sometimes, when I'm someplace new, my hand will find the scar under my hair. It's a scar like a bird. Her house looks big from the outside, but on the inside it's small like ours. She wouldn't be considered an attractive woman, in the city. She'd be a strange woman, or a coarse woman, or something else, but here, with the dog and the toolsheds behind the vegetable patch and the hens and the trees, and the butcher's shop, here in the kitchen, she was a woman you wanted to take an interest in you. And then I thought I should stop staring and stop thinking about whether she was attractive or not. Stop looking at her breasts and looking at her neck and her nape and trying to figure out what it was I wanted from her or why. Come on, stop it. And then I thought it had been so many days, so many months, so long since I'd felt something tugging inside me, or found anything or anyone attractive, that then I said to myself, Go on, Oriol, just go with the flow.

And I sat down in the kitchen and she made coffee and asked: "So what do you do?"

And I was afraid she was going to ask me things I didn't know if I could answer. And I said to her, "I'm writing a novel." Like the joke I make with my friends. And she said, "Yeah," and she didn't say anything more, she didn't ask what's it about or what do you write about, even though I had a really good reply worked up, and then I said, "I'm just kidding. I'm recovering." And she nodded slightly and lit the burner under the coffee and didn't ask recovering from what, either. She brought over some cups and a log, and I felt good, and when I felt good, the dog came over and I rubbed her snout, and her dark eyes looked at me generously and attentively and I asked: "How old is she?"

And she said, "Seven." And she said that Lluna was the daughter of another dog she used to have, daughter of yet another, in a long line of family dogs. And she said she'd had two litters, with neighbor dogs or wild dogs, and Mia told me she'd given all the puppies away, because she didn't want puppies around chewing things up and getting into everything, but that if Lluna got pregnant again, she would keep one, a female, she said, to continue the line.

"You live alone?" I asked, and then she said, "Yes, I live alone," and the coffee boiled and when she served it, I said, "I live with my mother," and she laughed a little. I hadn't had a cup of coffee since the accident, but I didn't say anything and I drank it. Then I thought if I was anxious that night, at least it'd be because of something good. And she sat down, and she asked, "So?" As if she was expecting me to ask her for something.

"Oh, it's nothing," I said, "I just came over to say hello."

"To get to know the neighbors." She laughed at me. I took a sip of coffee.

"What days do you work?" I asked.

"Tuesday through Saturday."

"No one buys meat on Monday," I said, and that amused her.

And then we talked for a long while, and we drank the coffee and we said a lot of things. One after the other, and it was strange, because she talked only about herself and about the dog, and she didn't say anything about anyone else, and it couldn't be that there wasn't anybody else, and I didn't mention anything about who I was before, or the accident, and that was crazy because everything I am now is because of the accident, and instead I told her, "One day I'll explain what I'm recovering from." And she lifted her coffee cup as if making a toast. And then I left and the dog walked me halfway.

From then on, on Mondays I would go see her. Late in the afternoon, because in the mornings I took walks with my mom, and Mia went walking with Cristina, a neighbor friend of hers. Sometimes I would go over on other evenings, when it wasn't a Monday, but when spring came Mondays were like the end of my week, like a gift or dessert, and sometimes with the coffee she'd give me cherries or loquats or peaches or almonds, and I didn't tell her I don't drink coffee, that I only drank it because I was at her house, and because I liked visiting her. And these visits were the most human and the most constant and the longest and the most peaceful interactions I'd had for so long, besides the time I spent with my mom. Mia has the equilibrium of embers, and it makes you calm, it makes you feel like laughing again, and drinking coffee, and makes you want the summer to arrive, and the autumn, or whatever it is that must arrive. Her face is like a tree, with two eyes like two ladybugs, and her mouth, hushed, and she just exudes peace, until suddenly she says something caustic as if there'd been a fire below the surface the whole time but I was only just noticing.

And then late one afternoon she pulled out a bottle of whisky and said, "Today we'll make carajillos." And I hadn't had whisky in forever, and I placed my hands on the table and she poured shots into our coffee. The whisky opened up a door inside me, and I told her how once upon a time Clara and I slept spooning in a bed. And once upon a time two men entered our home. And one had a gun and he forced us out of bed and made us kneel on the rug. And he pointed the gun at my head and I lowered my head like a little dog, and Clara screamed and the man screamed over her screams, wanting to scare us, but we were already scared, and with all that screaming and all that waving of the gun over my head, it went off, and the bullet entered and exited my skull. And then I take her hand and I place it on the bird that is the scar beneath my hair. And as she touches the bird I kiss her, and then she says, "I could be your mother." And another day she'll say, "I'm not your mother." Separated by all the things that happen in between. And if she'd had me at nineteen, or eighteen, I don't know, but I suppose I can imagine it, she could be my mother. But she never will be my mother, even if she wanted to and I wanted her to, but I don't want that and neither does she. I give her a kiss, and it's a kiss on the lips, and she kisses me back, and she holds me, and sometimes I'm like I was before. And other times it's like that other me never existed, as if everything escaped through that hole in my skull.

LLUNA

What I like best is when she whistles. With her fingers in her mouth. Because then I come running. I run as hard as I can, I jump, I fly like one of those little birds you just want to catch in your mouth, because they're pretty and fast, and then grind your teeth together and feel all their bones break. When she whistles I run over the grass and the fences and rocks. To the whistle. I fly over the grass and the fences and rocks. To the whistle, which comes out of her mouth, through her fingers. And I would run, I'd jump over the car if I had to, and over the house, if need be, and over every danger. Over and through and around all obstacles. Fast, because if she needed saving, I would save her from every bad thing. I would rip out the throat of any animal that tried to hurt her, any human who tried to hurt her, anything that made her little hairs stand on end, her heart beat too fast, made her sweat the sweat of fear. I would tear off their flesh in my mouth, and the blood would spurt and I'd keep biting and tearing, my snout hot with blood, and my fangs sinking deeper and deeper into flesh. That's why I run, mercilessly, to save her, because she's called me with a whistle and I understood her. Because I love her. Because when I get to her, I've saved her. And sometimes, when I get there, panting, she gently touches my forehead, and my back, and tells me I did good, and tells me sweet things I don't understand but I do understand. And all her love is in that touch, and all my love is in my running to save her.

The second thing I like is how her hands touch me. And the third thing I like are kids. The ones who walk. The ones who know all the games and laugh and have little hands that stroke you like clean flies. I like those kids who took the onions from the porch and threw them all onto the roof too. I like them all, even the newborns, like mushrooms, the ones they won't even let me look at. All of them, except for the ones who throw rocks at me.

She had harvested the onions from her patch. And she dried them on the table outside, all tied up and ready to hang. And the kids came. Like a party. They laughed, and I jumped all around them because they'd come to see me. That fun boy with a head round as a ball who smelled like bacon picked up the first onion. Like a game. And then all the others started grabbing them, too, and all the others threw them too. And if they threw me an onion, I would go look for it and bite it, and the onion juice got under my tongue, sour like puddle water. They threw the onions up high and even higher, because she wasn't home and it made them laugh. Because the onions were round and shiny and pretty, and because they got stuck up on the roof and smashed against the wall of the house, and because it was naughty and defiant, and because the whole yard was left covered in skins as if we'd eaten them all in one sitting, and because it was exciting to do and fun to watch. And I was so happy they'd come to see me, all the neighbor kids, who smelled like snacks and sweet juices, the kinds I'm not allowed to have, "No, Lluna, not for you, you can't drink this, this isn't for you." The days when she's not here are so long, so long they feel like a whole life. She always comes back, and I've learned that already, that she always comes back, but sometimes I still imagine she won't come back and then I worry. And I cry alone. I cry and cry and cry and no one hears me.

Once they ran out of onions, the kids left. I wasn't restless long because she soon showed up, and I thought, hip, hip, hooray! And I leaped with joy and she came out of the car and I was all eagerness around her legs and then I saw how mad she was. She looked at me first like it was all my fault. And then she saw the onions up on the roof. The onions smashed on the front of the house. And it couldn't be my fault. She walked through the skins and brought her hands to her forehead to block the sun and look up at the roof tiles, and looked at all the ruined onions that were stuck up there, and then I heard them, long before she heard them. The kids were coming back! They were coming back and this time they were speaking in soft, sad voices. And when I saw them, they were holding hands. They came with their heads bowed and were no longer laughing. They came and I wanted to play some more, I wanted to play with everybody, with the kids and with her, all at the same time. But the occasion required more severity on my part and I sat down. The kids came over and she went out to meet them, and the kids said they were sorry, they were sorry they'd ruined all the onions, they were so sorry, their little tails between their legs, for having thrown the onions onto the roof, and at the walls of the house and around the yard. And she told them things in the voice she uses when I can't help myself and I gnaw on shoes or taste some of the things she's thrown in the garbage. And then she made them pick up all the skins from the yard. And when the kids left, we decided we would forgive them.

The fourth thing I like is tasting things. I have to be stealthy and silent and clever when I try things, because she always says, "No, your dry food, your dry food, Lluna," and sometimes some bones, and some delicious wet food, but not melon, melon, no! And melon is the most refreshing delight in this universe and bread no, bread, no! And wine, no, and beer, no, and rocks, no, and poop, no, and I want to try it all, because everything has a taste and all the tastes are different, and even the things that are the same thing always have different tastes, and I want it all, even though she says, "No, not that, not that." I want it. They drink coffee and tell dogs, "No, you can't drink that," but I can drink anything. Coffee and liquor, juice and wine. Anything and everything. Today the man with the cane came and they are drinking coffee. And whisky. "No, not for you, Lluna, no . . . ," they say, and they laugh. And they keep laughing, and the more cups they swallow the closer they sit to each other. And they put their mouths together, she and the man, like someone drinking water from a spring, like somebody really, really thirsty and really hungry, and then they get up and they don't want any more coffee. When they aren't looking, I taste the coffee and the liquor, silently, not breaking anything, not making any noise, mmmmm . . . and I don't know anymore what I want: to drink coffee, now that they're leaving, or to gnaw on the cane, now that he has left it alone, or to go with them, now that they're headed to the bedroom. Should I taste the coffee, chew on the cane, or . . . We go into the bedroom. And then they uncover their skin, which they always have covered up with clothes, as if being all hairless like that is awfully cold, and then come the smells. The smells they give off are arousing and pleasing, and I like them and want to taste them. They are damp, moist smells, because in the dampness are all the smells. They take off their clothes quickly. Under their arms the smells are bitter and scratchy. In their sexes the smells are strong and pointy and stick in your nose and get on your tongue, and you want to smell them more and more, because the smell of sexes sets off your thirst and your curiosity and your desire to copulate. Butts smell fun and twisted up, much more interesting than the smell of feet, which is boring and actually smells just the same as shoes, which are more fun to chew for their rat shape than because they taste or smell good.

And then they touch each other with their hands. With the same hands they touch me with. And they caress each other, like the caresses they give me, but on the breasts, which are full like the ones on a cow and not like cats or dogs have, and on the butts, which are pale, the kind bald animals like them have. They caress each other with force and rhythm, like someone searching for something buried. And their sexes grow and turn red and the smell they give off is even better now and more moist. And I'm happy because they're happy, and because their hands are everywhere and the sounds are everywhere, and I want the smell to get deep inside my muzzle and stay there forever. I want a dog to come and for us to copulate too. And I go in circles to see them, and see their sexes, which are always hidden and when they aren't hidden they're small and calm and brown. And now they're swollen and wet and red, and they stick them inside each other, and they move, in and out, in and out, and now I see them and now they disappear, and now I see them and now they disappear, and they hug each other with their bellies, and not from behind, and I want to stick my nose right there where they are copulating because the smell is so good and it must taste so good, too, and then she says, "Lluna!" That's me! Lluna is me and only me! And they detach from each other and the smell invades everything, and she stands up and grabs me by the neck, and drags me. I would rather stay. I lick her bald knees, but she drags me out. And when I'm outside I already know she'll close the door, and she does close it. At first I stay behind the door because the sounds they make are pleasant and because my nostrils are still filled with the smell. But later I think that the breeze outside must be cool and I can already imagine the mice amid the grasses, coming out because the night is calm and cool. And I can already imagine the cats hidden in wait for them. And if there are hidden cats, malicious cats, annoying, ugly cats, disgusting cats, then someone's got to cast them out, someone's got to chase them, someone's got to kill them all.

IV

THE BEAR

I'm the bear this year. I'm the bear. We're the bears. We were sleeping for a very long time and now we are awake. We come to take what's ours. We come to reclaim it. We come to avenge what was ours and what they took from us. My claws strike the earth. Wake up, ye men who hunted us. My mouth opens, fierce, and out come the deep, hoarse roars of a rabid beast. Tremble in fear, men who killed us, men and women who flayed us and cast us out. And afterward, smug and calm, how you all laughed. You laughed because you were all so very brave. All of you, together. With those skinny white paws that kill treacherously. With those impotent little arms that kill treacherously. We were here first. Long before men and women. We came here first, and these mountains, this cold, this sky, this forest, this river and everything in it, fish and leaves, was ours. We were in charge. And then you came. Repulsive men who kill what you don't eat. Men who want it all, who take it all. You all came with your pusillanimous sheep, and your gutless cows, and your craven horses. I roar. And you plunderers built villages at the foot of the mountains and you claimed they were yours, the mountains. And that we were the outsiders, outsiders in our own homes. And then came the killing. Only lily-livered beasts kill what they don't eat. I scream louder and even louder, and I see, in the bottom of the valley, the village. Tremble, frantic beasts. Herd animals. Enemies. Cowardly, murderous flock. You look up at me, panicked atop the castle, you who've gathered. You all run this way and that, you bunch of chickens. I leap and I shout and I carry off a man like a sheep, down to the ground. Beneath the weight of my immense, stinking body, savage and dirty, he flails. I won't eat you, you trembling thing. Not even if I were dying of hunger and sadness. Not even if I'd just woken up from the longest winter and there was nothing left to eat in the world, no, I wouldn't eat you even then. I just want your fear. Scream. Louder. Scream! We roll along the ground and shots ring out. I'm blind with savagery. Blind with spleen. Blind with hunger after sleeping so long. Blind from the blows to the head, blinded to violence. Blind from my savage awakening. Damned village, my village. The hunger of the bears, when they awaken, will devour you all. It will devour you all. So proud you are. Laugh, while you still can. Scream, while you still can. The bears will awaken with the spring and it will be ferocious. A lush and deadly spring that will reclaim what is due, allied with the bears, and reconquer the plowed fields and the stacked rocks. The weeds will undo your works. The green will undo your works. The trees allied with time, the grass allied with death. Have no doubt, the day will come. Say your goodbyes. When the bears return and reclaim what's theirs, none of you will be laughing. When this drawn-out, blubbery winter ends, and we bears are not the sign of a propitious spring for you all, but rather of a spring that gets away from you. That corners you and casts you all out. You won't be singing again. I bellow. I roar like the accursed beast who controls me, who possesses me, deep within my very entrails. I am your fear awakening once a year. The shots sound out. The shots that are my friends. Like the villagers, who are my friends. Who would be my friends if I weren't the bear. Today I'm the bear and I have no mercy, not even for the old among you. I drink the fruit of the vine as if it were honey and tender berries. As if it were the blood of trout and sheep. As if it were the fear of those who die by my claws. I want more bodies beneath my body. I want kicks, and shrieks, and tumbling, I want bones and flesh, I want screams and sweat and punches. It's my duty as the bear. A bear has to be ferocious. A bear has to be feared and he must do his job well. Crazed with so much fear and so much rage and so much loneliness and so much humanity. The bear has to forget what he was before and what he will be after and just be a beast, become just the bear and the bear forever. I shout louder. Louder. Claws in the air, paws in the air, arms in the air. Terrible festival, beautiful festival, savage and accursed festival, the festival of my cursed village. My neighbors. My friends. You who chose me. I am the bear, thanks to you all. We are the bears, thanks to you all. We are fear because you all chose us. The huge honor of being chosen. I jump and roar from atop the castle. Before me, you all run, men and women. Behind me, you all hide, men and women and children. The little kids cry. The village opens like a mouth, and we reconquer it. I grab another man body, and I drink his fear. The village was ours before it was a village. I grab a woman body, and I drink in her panic. We reconquer the village just as the weeds will reconquer it, when the time comes. I roar. We reconquer the village just as we'll reconquer the mountain, when the time comes.

CRISTINA

I walk around with my face all blackened. Puffed up like a turkey. Sickly smug. Proud, as if my face were a flag made of soot and sunflower oil. Brandishing the emblem of my bravery after the battle. Damn Jean-Claude, and at the same time dear Jean-Claude. Fucking piece-of-shit Jean-Claude! And at the same time, my buddy Jean-Claude! He threw me down. He appeared in the middle of the crowd, with his three hunters, and he threw the stick to me twice. We were all singing: "Lala-lalalala, la-la-lalala!" Jean-Claude and I danced. This warmed my heart because it's rare they throw the stick to a woman. And I always say to him, "When are we going to have a woman bear?" And he responds, "That has to change." We danced, or something like it, jumping, like the kids, running, grunting, and throwing the long stick back and forth, all black and oily. My stomach was throbbing in my mouth. I could see my children out of the corner of my eye, terrified amid the scattered crowd, caught between the impulse to run away and the impulse to save their mother. And then Jean-Claude pounced on me, screaming like a madman, he forced me to the ground, dropping down first, like a big pillow of bones and filth, and he dragged my body down with his. The hunters shot into the air and the two of us rolled a good ten or twelve meters, downhill from the castle. My kids were hiding behind Mia and Alícia, who was recording the fall. Jean-Claude is a bear this year. And I strutted around in front of the pack the whole time, leading and fearless, to make sure he would see me and throw me down onto the ground. Finally a year when I'm friends with the bear!

When we come to a rolling stop, Jean-Claude smears my cheeks with black. The hunters come and squirt the wineskins into our mouths. They put more soot and more sunflower oil on his hands and he rubs it on his arms, face, and neck. They help me up. It's the Bear Festival in Prats de Molló. The hunters tell Jean-Claude whom he should attack now. They are all very drunk. We are too. I didn't remember how primitive and beautiful and fun and exciting it is, all at once. I hadn't been in years. Alícia had never seen it before. That's why I was leading the pack the whole time. So Alícia could see how they tackled me to the ground. So she could see how brave her wife was. Mia had come once before, with Jaume. Many years ago. But we don't talk about Jaume.

When the bear leaves, the kids come over to me and Pere says, "Mama, are you okay?" I kiss him to stain him with soot but the oil dries quickly and it's no longer easy to spread the black. Pere laughs and runs his hands over his face. Júlia touches her cheeks, too, and looks at everything with a mix of terror and amusement, as if we'd all gone crazy. My two precious kids. My two children, who came out from inside me at the same time, first one and then the other, like a drop of seawater and a drop of mountain spring water. Wrinkled and brown like two monkeys. Alícia would say, "You made us mothers, you made us mothers!" and she would hold their little backs with her hands as they nursed, one on each breast. Pere and Júlia laugh more, and cover their mouths, they keep going, and then they backtrack because one of the three bears is running around there. They grab at my sweater. Like they were little once again. "They're so crazy," they say. "Mama, you're being so crazy, too." A little bit proud. So intense. And I fill myself with the fresh, happy air of that afternoon.

After rolling around, seeing the three bears on the ground and watching the kids run, with that sky so blue, that air so fresh, and that sun so hot, I think we did the right thing, coming back. It wasn't an easy decision, but we did the right thing, coming back. My sister, Carla, and I both left this place, she left first because she's four years older, but we couldn't get away fast enough, leaving as soon as we turned eighteen. I was so tired of these mountains and my parents and these farmers and neighbors and these tiny little empty towns, no nightclubs, no museums that weren't all frigging Romanesque shit, no nothing. Drowning with so little going on. With more boxes filled with grenades and bullets and rifle pieces than could fit in the house. Drowning from all that up and down the mountain. Friendly mountains. Jean-Claude and I spent our teenage years like that, up and down, collecting bits of weapons. Because when you're fourteen years old, and fifteen, and sixteen, and seventeen, all you can do is think about fleeing. Getting away from here. Meeting people who've seen things. Real things. Seeing things yourself. You've hooked up with half the boys in this town and never felt a single spark. No interest in anything anybody here has to offer you. And this place weighing on you like a boulder, like a cow in your arms. Everything's so small, everything's all the same. I just wanted to be somewhere else. I just wanted a motorcycle, which, come to think of it, they never did buy me. I just wanted a car, and wind at my back! Don't let the door hit you on the way out. But you know what they say, east or west, home is best. And then one day, twenty-something years later, you're sitting at a table with your wife, you have five-year-old twins with mismatched eyes. Both of them. Gorgeous. One eye that's yellowish and one eye that's greenish. And Alícia says to you, "I think I could live there, in your town." Your gorgeous wife from Barcelona! And you think it over long and hard, and you think that you could, too, that you could come back home. The eighteen-year-old Cristina would try to strangle you, but you, at thirty-nine, you could. And your parents have always said they would fix up the top floor for you and your family. And the kids are little and it's not too late to change their school and uproot them. And you're tired of Barcelona, as tired as you can be of your little apartment in Sants. It was good while it lasted, but maybe it's time. Then they offered Alícia a job at the high school in Ripoll and that was that. Twenty-one years later, with her wife and kids, Cristina moves back home.

Júlia, who is the older twin by three minutes, loves history, like I do. This history that lies half-buried beneath our feet. And she's strong as an ox, this little girl, she never gets tired and she never complains, even after five hours of trekking up and down the mountain. But I can already see that when it comes to the grenades and weapons of the retreating soldiers, which is what I like, what I've collected all my life, she could take them or leave them. The Civil War, bor-ing. She's into the Iberian settlements. She's into the nails from Roman sandals. She's into the Celtic knife we found. "The ancients," as she says. The real old stuff. And then there's Pere, who has no patience, who wants it all here and now, but who can make you roll with laughter. Who tells me, "Mama, I want to go with you to find revolvers." Or Cris— sometimes he calls me Cris—and I don't know if I like that or not. "Cris, I want to go with you to find revolvers." And I tell him, "Revolvers are hard to find, what we might find are bullets or maybe grenades if we get lucky. If you go out looking only once every two years, you'd have to get incredibly lucky to find a revolver!" Perseverance is what fills up boxes. The second those fleeing soldiers thought about sitting down, the bullets would start falling on them. Grenades, too, all around. My hawk eyes, even when they don't want to, see the grenades and bullets. They haven't lost the knack. Even when the grenade looks more like a rock than the river rocks themselves. But revolvers . . . revolvers and pieces of machine guns and rifles are another story. They're like truffles.

I didn't realize how much I'd been missing all that. That I really liked all this stuff. After I left, I mean. That it wasn't just escapism, all that tramping through forests and collecting rusty weapons and bullets and grenades, belts and flasks, and all the things left behind by the sad, desperate people cross-ing these mountains after they'd lost the war. That was how I met Jean-Claude. In the forest. He did have a motorcycle and he went wherever he wanted to. We found each other in the middle of the forest. Really young. And Jean-Claude was so generous that he said, "Look what I found." First in French, then in Catalan. And he showed me a small revolver, pocket-size. Red with rust. Beautiful. So pretty that I wouldn't have shown it to anyone, not even my father. He had a revolver and I had a metal detector. I think he was more captivated by my metal detector than my charms. And we talked and talked, and looked for grenades and bullets and found them. Jean-Claude had never used a detector, and I taught him the song, that there's a beep and a tone and a sound that each metal makes. At the end of the day he gave me the revolver. I still have it. What a fool. He thought we'd end up together. And we did make out, we fooled around a few times, but, nah, there was nothing there. Now he's my kids' godfather. I spent years, from fourteen to eighteen, on the back of Jean-Claude's bike, no helmet, bouncing up and down the road. The two of us combing through the forests like goats and filling up boxes and boxes, the plastic ones from the bargain store, with bullets and grenades and pieces of guns. And when I left, I gave him the metal detector. I don't know if he was crying because I was leaving or because it was such a generous gift. Which is why, if my father now says he wants a drone, I want to buy him a drone. The ones that record. He could send it down the slope, down to the river, and crisscross the whole mountain, and "Oh the animals there'd be," and "Oh the things we'd see," he says. "To keep an eye on the lands and the roads," he tells me, as a selling point. And Pere tells him, "Grandpa, I bet you'll send the drone into the river the very first day!" My poor dad, he spent an arm and a leg on that metal detector for me.

We continue downhill with the soot-smeared crowd. Then we have to wait for all those people to get funneled into town, and Alícia puts her arms around my neck. "Let's practice," she said to me yesterday. "Cristina, if the bear throws me to the ground, I'll throttle you," she said. I laughed. The kids laughed. "Don't worry about that," I explained. "The bear only throws down people who want to be thrown, people he knows." We went down to the meadow, by the river, all covered with snow. A foot and a half. And today on the French side there was barely a trace. I played the bear. "Aaaaaggghhh," I shouted, and hugged them in a mortal embrace. I grabbed them with all the strength in my arms and I threw myself to the ground, letting them fall on top of me. They laughed like crazy. Adrenaline pounding in their skulls. "Aaaaaggghhh," I went. "Aaaaaaahhhh," they went.

Mia comes over and says, "Cristina, I really gotta pee." "Me too! All this beer! Kids, let's go peepee." But the twins don't need to. Alícia doesn't either. Mia and I break away from the crowd. We backtrack along the paving stones in the opposite direction from the bears. The lines at the bars are endless. We keep going downhill, cross through the square, where some people are drinking pastis to get their strength back up. The chestnut trees, the town hall. Before crossing the bridge we veer left, taking the downward slope that leads to the pool. There are cars parked everywhere. So crowded together they look like a barrier. "I can't hold it anymore!" exclaims Mia. We get behind a tall black Jeep. I pull out a little pack of tissues. One for me, one for her. We lower our pants and panties and we crouch with our white butts near the ground, and we piss two springs like two spurts that go pssss. The intimacy of the moment makes us giggle, and the voices in the background, and the face of the Jeep's owner if he were to catch us . . .

Not long after I came back up here, I asked Mia if she wanted to take walks with me, on Monday mornings. I like tromping through the forests, but strangely, I like it better with company. And I needed another friend up in these mountains, desperately. She looked at me as if I were from another planet. "To start the week off on a good foot," I said. I knew that the butcher's shop was closed on Mondays and I work from home and make my own hours. "Let's try it," she answered. And we tried it, and now we walk every Monday. Religiously. Even on Easter Monday. We didn't know each other well, Mia and I, before I came back. Not in a deep way. We knew each other as neighbors. From when we were kids. When I was a little girl, and she was a teenager and then a young woman. She was really pretty. A kind of pretty you might miss if you didn't look closely. I sort of wanted to be like her, pretty but brave, with thick, sensual arms, and I wanted to have a boyfriend like Jaume, who loved me the way they loved each other. Or not. Forget about Jaume. I liked Mia. I wanted her, crudely, even before I understood that desire. There's something very sensual about Mia. Very intimate. Something that makes you want her attention. I still like her, but not in a sexual way, not anymore. Alícia is my forever love. My endless love. The mother of my children. And now we're good friends with Mia. Even though one day she could say, suddenly, almost aggressively, very seriously, with a seriousness as cold as a knife: "No. I don't want you to talk about Jaume. It's a waste of time." And she'll leave you like that, with your heart jammed up into your throat, frightened when you realize you were trespassing. With a ton of questions to ask, like I have. Questions about the time they loved each other. About the thirst for love they sparked in me as a little girl. About Hilari's death. About where Jaume is now. And about whether they've ever seen each other again. All that curiosity making little trails inside me, like a persistent woodworm. Mia's smart, and she chose these mountains. And she doesn't complain. Even though that whole story with Jaume is a real shame. And Hilari's death, a punch in the heart. A fucking disaster. Best not to think of it.

But Mia and Jean-Claude are a hoot. When you get them together, I mean. When they come over to our place for dinner, and we sit for a long while after the meal, with ratafia, which Mia and Alícia pour down their throats without letting the bottle touch their lips, and Mia practices her French. They compare words. "How do you say finestra in French?" she asks him. "Fenêtre," says Jean-Claude. "Sure, fenêtre. Finestra, fenêtre, window. How do you say aixeta?" "Robinet." "That's so pretty, robinet." "You don't understand it, but you do, robinet." Jean-Claude and his saintly patience. And I insinuate with Mia, "So what about Jean-Claude, huh?" And she waves her hands as if shooing away flies. "Nah, nothing's going on with Jean-Claude." Mia's been seeing a young neighbor for a while now. She doesn't say much about it but sometimes I pass him, on Mondays, when we're coming back from our walk. Strange guy. Walks with a cane. Very handsome. Oriol is his name. And, hey, if she didn't seem happy, I would point that out to her. But she seems good, and I don't say anything.

She'd said something to me earlier, before she said, "No. I don't want to talk about Jaume. It's a waste of time." Mia had murmured, "We called you woodland elves and we pretended you were magic." And we both laughed, because we knew what she was talking about, with a childish, ashamed laughter. "We pretended you brought us luck." With the laughter of children running along the border between what they know, what they don't know, and what they intuit. She was dying of shame as she admitted they had let us watch. I was filled with shame admitting that we had watched them. She and Jaume would embrace each other and kiss each other and lick each other and take off each other's clothes, deep in the forest. And my sister, Carla, and I would hide and watch them. And we understood it and we didn't understand it. But if pressed, we would admit we understood more than we let on. They were so good-looking. And their skin was so pale, like slabs of marble. The way they moved awakened an emotion we still didn't know what to do with. It was a game. An education. An evolution of the game of spying on our parents, which turned into the game of spying on the neighbors when they went into the forest to grope each other. How embarrassing. But my confession about the espionage in the forest brought us together, as if we were friends growing up, and we shared something, a closeness, Mia and I. A firm, calm, warm affection, one that not even the coldness of "Stop. I don't want you to talk about Jaume. It's a waste of time" could rattle. "Okay. Fine. We won't talk about it," I said. "Let's talk about Jean-Claude," and that made her laugh and she gave my arm little pats. "Let's talk about the weather. Let's talk about my kids.

Let's talk about that writing group we've been saying we want to set up and never do."

When we finish pissing behind the Jeep, we go back up, toward the people, we look for Alícia and the kids. I'm happy. And a little drunk. I drape an arm over her shoulders and shake her. "Miaaaa!" I shout. "Cristinaaa!" she answers. Now come the barbers, all covered in white, and they'll shear the bears.

THE DANCE OF THE OAT HARVEST

I take another sip of beer. Fina doesn't like us to drink on the job, but Fina's not here tonight. And Quim—the other boss, and her brother—is always outside smoking and texting, and doesn't care what we do. I drink, because otherwise the hours don't pass. And Núria, who's up front at the bar, drinks, too, because if she didn't she'd end up busting beer bottles on the heads of the regulars who come to while away the evening. Now it's just Núria and me in the bar. I'm the cook. A few sausages and some loin chops and a couple of lamb chops and beans from a can and some grilled ham-and-cheeses and some eggs and home fries, and some salads, and then I clean up. And after I get it all spick-and-span, I leave the kitchen and serve beers to help Núria out. There used to be three of us. Núria, me, and the third wheel. The third wheel named Moi. Moi was from Sant Hilari. And he was a scumbag, the way he looked at Núria every time she turned around, and how he talked, and what he thought. One day I almost killed that scumbag and ended up back in prison. And, believe me, I didn't want to kill him. I was frying frozen breaded chicken and the scumbag was running around the kitchen, and there was no need for him to be in the kitchen, no need for him to stick his fingers into every saucepan and then pop them into that disgusting mouth of his. He should have been tending the bar with Núria. But, no, that idiot was always sticking his hands into everything, and always where he shouldn't be, like a hyena seeing what he can take, and obsessed with being in the way, like he was a boulder. He jostled me and the boiling oil in the pan spilled onto my leg, there's still a scar. And I went crazy with the pain and the stinging and the rage. And I thought, This will be the first and last time you burn me, you son of a bitch, and the last time you come into my kitchen with that rat face. And I gripped the pan's handle with both hands, and I smashed it against the kitchen wall as hard as I could. To scare the shit out of him. I didn't want to hit him. I swear I didn't want to hit him, I wanted to scare the shit out of him. And I smashed the pan against his back instead of smashing it against the wall. With all my fury. With all my rage. And he fell to the floor. Like a sack. As tall and greasy as he was. I thought I'd killed him. And I thought, Fucking hell, holy shit, Jaume, what've you done? And I saw a dark path, plastic chairs and gray police stations, and the ugly gait of the cops and the slouching way the guards walk, and thick glass, and filth in the corners, and tiles like in a school, or in a hospital, but a million times sadder, if that's possible. And then he moved. If I had hit his head or his neck, I would've killed him. He was screaming like a chicken. He was screaming like the hyena he was, like a mule, he screamed and screamed and screamed, "You're crazy, you're crazy, you're fucking nuts, motherfucker," he said, his eyes bulging out of their sockets, terrorized, so scared he must not even have felt the pain. And then, with the pan in my hand in front of him, I thought there were two things I could do. Back off and apologize, and he'd tell Fina and Quim, and that would be the end of that job, and let him humiliate me, and have to ask for his forgiveness every day for the rest of my life. Or I could keep going, just continue, take it a few steps further, I hadn't actually killed him, and he wouldn't be able to move for a week but he was alive for fuck's sake. So I just knelt down, and whispered into his rat ears: "The next time you come into my kitchen, I'll kill you." And he said, "You're crazy, you're crazy, you're fucking crazy," and the next day he quit. And now it's just me and Núria behind the bar. Fina comes by every so often to bark orders and drink gin and tonics. And Quim comes for beers, to smoke outside and send messages to women. And we're fine.

I swallow another gulp of beer. I make the best dinners for myself and Núria. Unlike all the other restaurants in the world, where they give employees pasta and rice as if they were pigeons, to fill bellies on the cheap. No, now that it's just me and Núria for dinner, I make us nicer meals than I do for paying customers. I make her salads with vinaigrettes and sometimes I buy a duck breast just for us. Pay for it out of my own pocket, if I have to. Or I save the darkest steak for her. And I tell her not to smoke so much, shit, as if I were her mother. She's not even twenty-five, why the hell is she smoking so much? We all smoke here like the ban in bars and the horrible warnings on the packs never happened. Thirteen-year-olds smoke here, like idiots. We even smoke inside the bar after we close, around three. A few of us stay inside, or it'll be just me and Núria refilling the fridges, and then we smoke and drink. And even I smoke, as much as it disgusts me. But I wake up early in the morning no matter what. Whether I've been drinking and smoking or not. I get up to walk and do what needs to be done. If you don't get up early and walk, these late-night jobs will rot your soul. Just the drinking and the smoking and the pitiful stories. It's worse than prison. Even though that's not true. Even though you shouldn't say that. There are good things about this place, the Montseny range, first and foremost. Matagalls, the Agudes, all the springs . . . Second, the people, they're good folks, and even the losers who come to the bar are okay. Fina knows I was in prison for murder, and in most places that would be enough to keep you from getting a job, but not here. Third is being able to go where you want, whenever you want, even if you don't end up going. Choosing when you get up and when you shit and when you eat. If you can't choose that, your life is half a dog's. That's why I don't have a dog, and I do like animals, but a dog is a prisoner of his owner and can't choose when he eats or when he shits. And on top of it all he's forced to love him. I take another sip. This mountain isn't like the ones at home and at the same time it's more like them than a lot of other mountains are since they're both in the same region. Oh, right, I was thinking about the people, the people in this godforsaken place, they're good folk. I flip the sausage I'm cooking for Miquel Gras and drink some more. Even Fina, who doesn't let me drink, she's a good woman when she's not being a killjoy, she's even fun to be around, and here I am, and the years keep passing and everything's fine. Miquel Gras, he should just stuff his mouth with sausages and beans or whatever, and quit talking shit all the time, seems like he only opens his mouth to start shit, just to get so-and-so mad at somebody else, just to say shit that's none of his business, and what so-and-so said about somebody else and what that somebody else did wrong. He's just dragging a whole wheelbarrow of bullshit and misunderstanding along behind him like a train. But Miquel's got two sons and two daughters and a bunch of grandkids, so he had to sell his car and buy a van, and I figure if that whole string of sons and daughters and grandkids love him, well, then there must be something good under that coal-black tongue of his. And I pull his sausage off the grill. Montserrat's here today, too, she had a sandwich of pork loin and cheese, and three little plates of olives all for herself. Montserrat laughs at all the jokes, except the ones about her retirement. Whether she's gonna retire or not, how she had a party to celebrate her retirement months back even though she kept working. When you joke about it she gets furious and leaves without paying and she'll settle up the next time she comes in, and the day she comes back in, you won't even remember the joke and she'll still be mad. And then there are all those young'uns, they're not bad kids at all. Some are worse than others. But mostly they just come in to chat and watch soccer and drink one beer after the other, and eat, now that's what I call eating, only the ones coming from practice really eat, the ones who can't help themselves, they come in just starving. And they always want hamburgers. A few kids died maybe a year ago now, and the town hasn't gotten past it. When people start talking about it, you know how people like to talk about sad, morbid shit, well, I just leave. Because they were all drunk, bouncing around in a car, and they went off the road and crashed and all five of them died. And this town is small enough that everybody knew at least one of them, and if you didn't, you knew their dad or their sister. I can just imagine them, in the car, all laughing and smoking and joking around, all that blood in those veins that'd never really known suffering, all that fun, and so alive. I think about the last thing they must've said before the car went all swervy and then, bam. A few moments of pain, a few moments of fear, maybe, and then that was it.

Núria comes into the kitchen and says: "Jaume, don't you fall asleep in here," and she smiles in that way that throws me off and I don't know how to respond. "Two steaks with fries for Assumpta and Marc from Can Sala."

And I say, "Your wish is my command." And then I feel totally stupid and ridiculous. She is swallowed up by the plastic curtains.

I peel and cut up the potatoes myself, and leave them soaking in water overnight. I pull the steaks out of the fridge, with watery red blood, and before I put them on the grill I go out for a sec to say, "Hand me a beer."

Núria's good like that, she doesn't judge. She doesn't get riled up about that sort of stuff. She grabs the beer, opens it and hands it to me, and keeps on doing what she was doing. She has her moments, her hard-ass jokes, with that fox face of hers, but fucking with you for drinking at work or driving drunk, nah. "Thanks," I say, and I put the steaks on the grill. The Salas, who ordered the steaks, are nuts. Pair of hippies who came to the Montseny to smoke weed, you never know what to expect from them. Sometimes they fight and scream at each other and it looks like they're about to start throwing chairs, and other times they just laugh and drink and get in the car and drive over to Vic or Girona to go out and party, and it's not like they're young either.

And then there's Genís, with his white socks and his shoes, and you have to watch how many beers you serve him, because he's a good guy but you can't let him drink too much. He's around forty, or older, no one knows, because he looks like a little boy and he's got a little-boy mouth. His parents are old, old enough for him to be forty, but Genís seems like he's nine or ten or at most eleven. Núria told me one day that after the first beer all the others she gives him are alcohol-free and that she doesn't charge him for half of them. Genís goes everywhere on foot, and you always run into him walking around, and sometimes you say, "Do you want a lift?" And sometimes he'll get in and other times, even if it's raining, he won't.

And then there's Carmeta, she's the one I like best, Carmeta, who's missing an arm, and is all joyful and slow and kind, as if having one less arm has made her life easier instead of harder. And Carmeta drinks vermouth, and sometimes she comes in with her brother or her sister, both of them with long arms and a dusty grief inside. And when she's celebrating something she orders cockles. And then there are the men who make buses at the factory, who all shout as if they're used to talking over the sound of the machines. They start with beers and then move on to whiskies and patxarans and mixed drinks. And sometimes families come in, but early, and the kids share an order of steak and fries and the parents eat without talking much. Young couples never come in. As if they were embarrassed to love each other or something, I don't know.

When it's two minutes to midnight, I close up the kitchen. I like cleaning the kitchen, because I'm preparing everything for another day, and when it's clean and you look at it, all polished and shiny, it makes you feel good. I learned all I know about cooking in prison. And I learned it pretty well. I'm good at it and I enjoy it. Valentí, he was the one who taught me, would say that cooking is like singing, there are those who are born knowing how, like a gift, but with a little bit of effort anyone can do it. I don't know if it's the best example. I already knew how to cook a few things for my dad by the time my mom died, but with a bit of technique, with a few basic skills, you can do wonders.

I finish cleaning up, I go out to the bar, and Guifré shows up. Always at the last minute and always just him and his shadow. And he tells me he has a story about bears for me. And I say, "Oh yeah? Let's hear it." Because that's the joke, some people around here call me the Pyrenees bear. They're just jealous, with their tiny pimple of a mountain while I've got a whole mountain range. And sometimes they don't even call me by my name, they just call me the Bear. I actually like when they do that, because it makes me think of home and of Mia. And at the same time I don't like it at all, because it's like a stab under my armpit to think about home and about Mia.

The bear story he told me goes like this:

"Once upon a time there was a blacksmith, who was irascible, hairy, strong, and corpulent, like you," he says, "who lived alone, and was always angry and always cursing, so much so that when he picked up his hammer, the iron would already start to tremble, and when he had to shoe an animal, it would hold its breath.

One day, a vagabond showed up in the blacksmith's town, dirty and barefoot. He went over to the smithy and he asked for some alms. The blacksmith, from the forge, shouted: 'Put on some shoes, you animal, and begone!' as he threw a red-hot horseshoe at him.

"The beggar, without moving, stared at him and exclaimed:

"'A bear you are and a bear you shall be!

And you shall climb every tree,

save the hawthorn, too prickly,

and the fir tree, too slippery.'

"And the blacksmith immediately turned into a bear and ran off growling to the forest, because that beggar was Our Lord."

Guifré explains that all bears are descendants of that blacksmith, and that's why they walk upright like people and climb every tree except the hawthorn and the fir. I laugh when I hear him say "Our Lord" and I pour him a draft beer. The rest of the night passes quickly, and Núria, who has me behind the bar and can go out every once in a while for a smoke, is happy. Quim the boss left a while ago, so we use beers to treat our thirst and our boredom and our desire for the shift to be over with. And when I start to feel bloated, we switch to gin and tonics. Everybody's had a good day, everybody's relaxed, nobody wants to pick a fight, or complain, or any stupid drunken bullshit, and everybody leaves when it's time to go home.

When we lock the door from the inside and lower the blinds halfway, Núria lights a cigarette and leaves it in the ashtray on the bar. She goes down to the storeroom with the hand truck to get four cases of long-neck beers. She comes back and grabs the smoke and takes a drag. She puts the full plastic cases onto the wooden bar, gets behind it to load up the fridges, cigarette in her mouth and her gaze like a fox. She's got the gaze of a fox who likes to play around with her victims before she kills them. And I can tell she's itching to pick a fight, and she asks, out of nowhere, "What about you, Jaume, what's your story? Where're you from?"

I'm putting the chairs up on the tables, and I answer, "From up in the Pyrenees. Like the bears."

She already knows that much. She puts down her cigarette and places the bottles in the fridge in the shape of a pyramid.

"My mother was a water sprite," I say then. And I think about my mother, who spoke so little, with that tranquil smile she had, good as gold, when she was happy, it made you feel so good to make her laugh, even though her smile showed her missing front teeth. My mother, all her kindness squandered. My mom, who died before the accident, and I'm so, so glad of that, that she died before it all went down. I go over to the bar, like I'm a regular. I'll sweep up, but first I pick up her cigarette from the ashtray, because I've finished putting up the chairs. She asks, "Are there water sprites in the Pyrenees?"

"There are sprites everywhere."

"How do you know she was a sprite?"

I gesture with one hand for her to pour me another gin and tonic and I tell her another truth. "When my mom and dad got married, my mother made him promise he would never say out loud that she was a sprite. But when I was born, I was so ugly that my father couldn't believe I was his son, and he said, 'What was I thinking, marrying a water sprite!' And, poof, my mother disappeared and we never saw her again."

"It's always the same story with water sprites." She smiles.

She pours two gin and tonics. I keep her cigarette and she lights herself another.

"You know what I think about secretive, mysterious men who keep everything to themselves?" she asks. "I think they're empty like a shell, and don't have anything to say."

I lift my head, and she looks at me with eyes that smile combatively, capable of so many better things than being here. The eyes of a fox, bored of the boys in this town, and the cars of the boys in this town, and the views and perspectives in this town. I have nothing to offer her, and I don't want her to look at me like that, with her mouth slightly ajar like a door, so I say, "I killed a man."

I say it without looking at her, because I don't want to see her reaction. She changes position, smokes, and waits.

"I killed a guy who was my friend. By accident. We were hunting and I shot him in the back. My shotgun went off. Up in the mountains, so high up that he died in my arms and it took me hours to carry him down."

There you have it, a secret like a treasure. A little jolt to the soul. A story to ponder, an anecdote to tell your friends. A truth like a rotted fruit. A sad scene.

Then I look at her and say, "And I spent some time in prison."

She is still as a fox.

There are things that remain etched in your soul. Article 545 of the 1973 Penal Code. Five years. Three years provisional and two sentenced. That's how it is when you live right beside the fucking French border. No one believes you won't take the ten steps across it to avoid five years in a cage. And I can recall everything, one thing after the other, almost without pain. What I remember least is Hilari. Hilari dying. The blood and the hair. I barely remember how I got him out of the forest. Or the faces of the civil guards, or the first night in jail, or the second. And then I'm at Pont Major penitentiary awaiting trial, and then the trial happens and I don't care about anything anymore.

And she asks, "What was prison like?"

I say something random, and make a gesture sort of like a smile and I ask, "Can I take a beer with me?"

She wants me to stay and tell her more secrets, and to do something with this night, because it will be a night to remember, better than a lot of others, because tonight we're alive and we're here at the bar, in front of each other. But I don't want to stay, and I don't want to think about prison, and I don't want her to look at me with that ajar-door mouth, and she hands me a beer and I ask if I can leave, if she minds closing up alone. My father died during the second year. Before my trial. It's like a goddamn well. You shouldn't open the door to memories, because there's nothing good inside there.

The car is waiting for me in the dark and I get inside and it smells like a little house. I drive toward the edge of town instead of toward home, because the night is cool and the beer is cool and the curves in the road are the promise of some comfort. A little comfort, please. I step down hard on the gas, and I take the curves like I'm dancing, like I'm escaping. The road is black, the median like a necklace, an ornamental border that goes through it all like the skin of a snake. And the forest opens up before me, yellow and gray, as if I were a knife. The sky is lighter than the forest and the road, because the sky has the light hidden beneath it. I open the windows and the good night slips into the car. There are no other cars on the road because the cars are sleeping. The golden water slides quickly from the neck of the bottle and it's a field of barley. A field of wheat. A field of oats. The dance of the oat harvest. *The dance of the oat harvest I shall sing to you, the dance of the oat harvest I shall sing to you, my father as he sows it, over here, over there; he bangs on his chest* and then there is a huge bang. The violence of a body crossing into the car's path makes a horrifying thud. Holy shit. My hands—electric with shock—grip the steering wheel and the beer, which goes flying, spills all over the floor. The car stops and the darkness grows hushed in atonement. I feel myself breathing hard and I could cry with the fear of not wanting to see what it is I killed. In front of me the road is clean. The trees turn as if looking at me, and I remain still for a moment, with my back to the darkness and death.

When I get out of the car, I can see right off it's an animal. And when I get a good look at the roe-deer in the middle of the road, red, lit up by the car's taillights, I shout, "God!" over and over and really loud, and then I say, "Fuck!" over and over and really loud, and then, "Fucking hell," and when I kneel down by the animal and put my hand on its forehead and between its ears, I think how it's the roe-deer. I know, I know it's not that roe-deer. But I think it's the roe-deer that Hilari and I didn't kill. The beer ricochets off the walls of all my veins, and the memories that flood in afterward ricochet off the walls of my skull, and I take the animal in my arms, just like how I carried Hilari. I never told Mia I was sorry. I didn't allow any visitors. I didn't go back when they let me out. I open the rear car doors and the dead beast weighs more than you'd think, with how light it is when it's running, on those thin little legs. I'm careful not to let him bang against the door frame, those knees and those hooves that hold up all that flesh. I have to get in from the other side, to pull the animal in by its neck, which is hard and thick and fibrous and hot. His two back legs slip, inert, off the seat, outside the car, and I go back to the first door and grab its haunch and lift and push it into the seat, without blood, it wasn't even bleeding. It's Hilari's roe-deer, and I never told Mia I wanted her and I was sorry. How could anyone ever forgive me, if Mia can't forgive me? I close the doors and I know that all the animals of the night are watching me, bewildered and terrified, from the darkness, with their eyes lowered so the gleam doesn't give them away.

Sometimes words don't come, and not even a thought comes. The only thing is the doing with your hands, like turning the keys that are still in the ignition, which is a simple thing, and releasing the hand brake and putting the car into first, which is easy and mechanical. The roe-deer like a child sleeping in the back seat. I would have wanted to have kids. With Mia.

The road stretches out before me. The empty beer bottle clinks on the floor. The place of the accident, in the morning, will seem like a different place. It'll take me an hour and a half. An hour and fifteen minutes if I drive fast. I drive fast, so air will rush in hard through the window and make that noise that fills my ears and mixes with the acrid smell of the forest, and of wild game, and of fear and death and my sweat and the sweat of the beast fermenting, getting only stronger and more sour and more frightened. I turn on the radio so it can keep me company. And that's when I feel them, even before I find a station.

Deep, like the dark holes that reach the depths of the earth. I feel them on the nape of my neck, like two fingers. I feel them long before I see them, and long before I understand them, and it takes me a while to locate them, and then I turn and there they are, the two of them, the open eyes, like two wells, of the roe-buck. Wet and black.

THE GHOST

The moon is round and full, and Lluna lies at the foot of the bed, and we go to bed early because we're tired. I don't let Lluna sleep up on the bed, and if she wakes me up in the morning because she's feeling impatient or hungry or overflowing with love, I get angry or I pretend I'm angry so she won't keep doing it.

I get into bed and say goodnight to her, and I don't see her, but I know she's lying down with her snout resting on her front paws, and a resigned expression. She doesn't take long to fall asleep.

"It's been a few years since I've been with anybody," I tell him. Like I told him the first time. And he keeps kissing me. I thought I was over all this stuff, that I didn't need somebody else to give me my pleasure, that I hadn't missed any of it. But now that my desire is stirring, deep inside, I cling to it because it's blooming and fun and I want it to grow. Oriol says, "Me too," like the other time. And I laugh, because it can't be. And he laughs.

His hands are firm as he caresses me. After all that trembling I didn't think they could grab anything so firmly. His mouth tastes of alcohol, of a wine reduction that's been used for cooking, and he has lips, and his lips want me and his arms gather momentum, and I'd imagined I would be in my head, thinking about each gesture, thinking about every single thing that happened as it happened. But no. The blood, his hands, my hands, they just flow, taking the lead, faster, deeper, and we remove our clothes and we touch each other, and it had been a very long time since I'd touched a man's penis. And then Lluna, who always does the same thing, licks my knee with a cold, alien tongue and muzzle. I get up and take her out of the room and I come back quickly so everything will go back into place, and I don't want him to stop, I want him to go in again and out again, and I look at him and I smile at him and he looks at me and he goes farther inside, and it is the first time, this one, the first of the many times that will come after.

Oriol is never the same thing. When he makes love he's a silent thing that knows how to caress. A whole man and good company. But sometimes, after making love, he's a broken man who wants to talk about the thieves who entered his home, and about the hole in his head, and about before and now. I listen and I never say anything about Hilari, because he is telling his story, and because his story is the only story he wants to be heard. And because I don't want to talk about Hilari. Hilari is my story.

Sometimes, before making love, he has a day of big words, of talking about books and playing at cold, highbrow detachment. Those times, I bustle about and barely speak, so it seems like he's conversing with a rock, and I go out into the garden or the vegetable patch and I water the flowers, and when he grows tired of pretending, I grab him and we take off our clothes.

Sometimes, when he leaves, since he never sleeps over, and I've never asked him to, I think: Mia, what did you want? What were you expecting? Not about him not sleeping here, that's fine. About the whole thing. He's a handsome young guy, what's he doing up here with his mother and a cane and hands that tremble? And then I think: You weren't expecting anything, Mia. And that's fine. And I let him visit me. Because I like his visits. I never visit him, because whatever his mother thinks of me, good or bad, I'd rather she not think it in front of me. And because he knows where I am and he can come when he wants to and I don't have to guess whether he's having a calm day when he's good company, or whether he's having a day of closing himself up like a walnut.

Hilari was always the same thing. He was like the early morning air. Cool and thin and full of ideas and energy and possibility. But always like the morning air. Never like the heavy air of afternoon. Never like the sluggish air at midday, the blue air at dusk, or the dark night air. My mother was like Oriol, so fickle. You never knew if she'd start singing at you or scold you. And then, when she got old, with the sickness, you didn't know if she'd be a little girl or an old woman, a mother or a daughter, if she'd recognize you or think you were her auntie Carme or who knows what. Grandpa Ton was always the same thing. But it was a boring thing. Boring like broken tools. Like a light bulb that's really burned out, with no blind man to switch it off. And Jaume was also always the same. A brown bear of the Pyrenees. But there are none left, in these parts.

When we're done making love, Oriol says to me, "I'm going to till the vegetable patch. I'm going to make irrigation lines. I'm going to tie up the tomato plants."

And I think how the tomatoes in my garden are always green and small and ugly, and I stay stretched out in bed for a little while. It feels good to not do anything, not say anything, and not look at anything, after making love. There are flashes of lightning. The white light splatters everything like spit-up milk. I don't hear the thunder. When there were thunderclaps, my mother would shout, "Domènec!" A shriek. One "Domènec!" for each clap of thunder. Not for the lightning, which was what killed my father, but for the thunder. And then she would cry and pray, and she would make us all kneel and pray that no lightning would hit the house.

When you see a flash of lightning, you have to count the seconds. The seconds between the lightning and the thunder. If the interval is brief, between the lightning and the thunder, it means the lightning hit close by. And you have to find shelter. But never under a tree. And you should never run, because lightning likes gusts of air. And you must never get close to the electrical poles, or the animal fences, or isolated rocks, or caves. You shouldn't ever get in the river during a storm. And if you're at home, it's best to close the windows and doors and turn off the lights, and not start a fire, because lightning likes fires.

I hear Oriol rustling around outside, and I go out to keep him company. The moon is over the vegetable patch and Lluna lies in front of the patch, and he has his back to me and is digging, weeding hoe in one hand, and he's waking up the earwigs and the ladybugs and the little lizards and the worms and the other little sleeping beasties with his methodical blows, with his turning over the earth. I tell him, "I've come to keep you company."

He turns. And he is Hilari. And he says, "Wonderful, Mia."

And I'm so happy he's not Oriol anymore and that he's Hilari now, because Hilari is better company than Oriol, so much better company than any other company, and because I miss him so much, Hilari, I miss him every day.

And he says, "Bring over the hose, we can do some watering now that the sun's down."

And I bring him the hose. The night is pleasant, I don't want it to end.

Hilari never wanted to be alone, he never wanted to do anything alone, he would say, "Mia, do you wanna keep me company while I poo?" Or, "Will you come with me to gather wood?" Or, "Let's go look at the river." And you would always go with him. As if he was afraid to be alone even for a little while. "Will you keep me company, Mia?" he would say. "Will you keep an eye on me, Mama?" he would ask Sió. As if he would evaporate if you weren't watching. Jaume, on the other hand, went everywhere alone. He would walk for an hour to get to school and then he would walk back up an hour and a half to get home. All by himself. Until Hilari caught up with him. Hilari, who was good with wild animals because he was patient, adopted him. He kept him, like you'd keep a little field mouse, or a sparrow that fell from its nest. And after that the three of us went everywhere together, because Jaume never got tired, and he never said no to anything. And he didn't mind taking a bit longer to get home in exchange for a little company, some little game that warmed his belly, like stone soup.

In the beginning it bugged me to have the Giants' son hanging around. So slow and so devoted. He showed up one day and from then on he showed up every day. And sometimes he called Hilari "brother." Because he didn't have any, no brothers, no sisters, no friends. As if Hilari were everybody's brother. I didn't like that. Because he was my brother, mine alone. And Jaume would call me "M-i-a." He would say Mia with an emphasis on every letter, and really slow. And I didn't like him. I didn't like him, because it took him longer than Hilari to get things. And because Hilari had patience for him and I didn't, and it made me look mean. And because I would get tired of him tagging along all the time and having so little to say, as if we'd adopted an old dog.

But then one day Jaume told us that his father was half man and half giant, and that his mother was full giant. And I looked into his eyes and I saw that he wasn't an old dog, he was a bear. His parents raised horses and sheep and made cheeses, and sold them at the market before his mother died and his father locked himself up at home to eat only dried food or preserves and pickles. His parents were strange. They were old, and missing teeth, and they didn't talk much and they didn't know how to read or have any book-learning, and they were surly, I suppose they got tired of people laughing at them. They lived high up, really high up. And people made fun of them because they were both tall and big, they looked like siblings, and they had strong, French-inflected accents that were hard to understand. People called them the Giants. And when they called them the Giants they also meant that they were dim-witted, that they were siblings who'd married and had a dim-witted son, and it was cruel. But when Jaume said it, that his parents were giants, I looked at him and I got the joke and his cleverness. And all of a sudden, just like that, it stopped being him that followed us around, we were the ones who always wanted to be near wherever he happened to be.

Another day he said his parents had made him out of snow. And I loved that story. His parents weren't able to have children, he explained. And they were sad. Then one year, in the late autumn, when the first snow fell, his mother made a snowman in front of their door and she sewed baby clothes for it and dressed it. But when night fell, his mother felt bad leaving the snow baby outside in the snow, and she picked it up and brought it inside the house and placed it in front of the fireplace. And with the fire's warmth, the snow baby thawed and took on the color of a person and then moved its eyes and then its arms and legs and turned into a boy, and they named him Jaume.

And it all started very gradually and very securely, like a stone bridge. As if it had to last forever. As if forever was then. And the evenings were languid, and languid were the weather and the woods. I'd help out at the butcher's shop, and carry the money folded up in newspaper, and give it to my mother. Hilari helped Rei out in his vegetable patch, and he would bring green beans and zucchini and tomatoes and endives and potatoes. Our grandpa had died by then, without saying a word, gently, gently. Jaume made cheese and smelled of goat. We still had time to make forts, and to hunt rabbits with noose snares and to play at making magic potions and cannelloni from cattle feed and to try to ride cows or start a fire without matches or to eat wild strawberries until our bellies were bursting.

And sometimes we held hands, Jaume and I, because it was fun to have a hand inside yours. Or we would give each other massages and tickle each other's arms, just for the pleasure of touching. And Hilari didn't get mad. Hilari never got mad unless you left him alone. And we weren't embarrassed to hold hands in front of him, or braid each other's hair and tickle each other, and if he asked us, we'd do it to him too. We knew that people in love kissed each other on the mouth, and slept hugging each other and made babies, but we were in no rush, not yet.

And then I turned fourteen and I quit school and went to work at the butcher's shop every day. I told my mother that when Manel, the owner, retired, since he didn't have children, we would buy the butcher's shop with the money she kept hidden behind a tile, from when we sold the empty house in Camprodon that belonged to Grandpa and Great-Aunt Carme. And I told Jaume that, and I told him we would sell his cheeses too. And Hilari said we would sell the farm animals, and eggs, and that he would give me the boars and hares he hunted, and if we cooked them, we could sell them that way too. I said, "Okay, sure," I said yes to everything. And then my mother started to say I shouldn't go into the forest with the lads because they were only thirteen years old, and I was now a woman. I wasn't interested in being a woman. With all the cruelty of womanhood and the few things left to you once you become a woman. But I went with them anyway, they would come pick me up in the evenings when I finished at the butcher's and we would go to the town festival, and for hikes, and hunting, and everything.

And then, when we were fifteen or sixteen, I'm not sure when exactly, the desire to kiss each other awoke inside me and

Jaume. Sometimes Hilari would get tired of our moist noises, as he called it, and he would go home to help Mama. Hilari would leave and the woodland elves would show up. They'd whisper and laugh softly, like magic. Jaume tasted soft and deep and salty, like salami. And we tried all the nooks and crannies and all the ways, and it was a new smell, the smell of kisses. He would carry me on his back deep into the forest, and I would say, "I'm riding the bear, I've tamed a Pyrenees bear!" And then he would roar and run and drop me gently down to the ground and get on top of me, grunting. I would laugh, from the adrenaline, from the tickling of the air that came in and out of his nose as he sniffed my hair and neck and mouth and belly, and from his grunts and growls, and his growling awakened our desire to make love.

And we loved each other for all the years that would come after, and even though they passed very quickly there were a lot of them. Until the accident.

And then in my dream Hilari says, "Mia, tell me about how Mama got lost."

And he takes off his T-shirt and tears it into strips to tie up the tomatoes. And I cry out, "Hilari, don't rip your shirt, I have old sheets in the house!"

"It's an old shirt," he says.

We tie up the weak, green tomato stalks with the shirt strips, and I tell him, "She got lost and I imagined the forest opening up its mouth. Mama with her purple robe getting under the trees like into a wolf's throat. Following the footpath like a length of intestine that leads to the hole where everyone who the mountain eats ends up. Papa and you, Hilari. But the forest spit Sió out"—I can't help but giggle—"like it couldn't chew her up. Too leathery, that mama of ours."

And we laugh.

"Like when your meat would ball up in your mouth and Mama would grind your steaks and loin chops and make little mountains for you," I continue. "Like the story that Papa would tell her, about the woman who wasn't a good wife because she didn't know how to do anything, and her husband sent her back to her parents, and told them he would come back for her once they'd taught her. The forest didn't want her. It gave her back to me so I could take care of her, sick as she was with her head like a junk drawer, filled with odd and scattered memories. And we called for her, and Lluna barked and barked, and half the town went searching for her and then the cops and the firemen showed up, looking for the missing person. We published messages on Facebook and notices in the newspapers and we put up signs on trees all over Molló and Camprodon and even Beget and Ripoll, with the photograph from her ID, and got no response. She spent two whole nights in the forest, and then she came back, on the third morning, and said she had slept with the water sprites. She told me she'd slept with the water sprites! And I said, 'Mama,' and she said, 'I don't care if you don't believe me, if you were a little girl you'd believe me.' And they kept her in the hospital, doctors in and out looking her over and not a scratch to be found. But she didn't tell the doctors anything about the sprites. I threatened her, saying that if she got lost again I'd put her in a home, but there was no need, because her time to die came soon after that."

I tie up another tomato plant and continue, "One time she hit us, because we told her we'd seen water sprites. You remember that, Hilari? She told us to stop with the lies and foolishness."

Hilari grabs a strip of torn T-shirt and makes another bow that hugs the tomato stalk to a stake. His smile is focused and broad as he listens to me, his chest and back bare and his head turned to one side, because Hilari loves to hear stories from when we were little.

"Remember the sign that you said we would use to communicate, if we died? If one of us was left alone?" I ask. "I can't remember the memory of the water sprites anymore. I imagine them like in fairy tales, pretty and washing out white clothing. But I can't see the memory of when we saw them. I remember how Mama hit us. But that's it. I remember how you said that we did see them and then you chose the sign we would use if one of us was dead. You had a lot of ideas and none of them worked. You would come and visit me as a ghost, you used to say. And I asked you, 'At night or during the day?' And you'd say, 'During the day if I can, and otherwise, at night.' And I said, 'No, not at night, Hilari, you'll scare me.' Then you suggested: 'In dreams!' But I'd say, 'In dreams we'd think we just dreamed it and that the other one wasn't really there, like when you dream about Papa.' And you said we could come in animal form, a fallow deer or a boar or a rabbit, and I said, 'Hilari, what if they hunted you?' Then you said, 'No, Mia, as some animal nobody hunts, like a cat. What if Ruda chased you?' Ruda was the dog we had before, Lluna's grandma. 'Well, then as a dog,' you said. 'How would I know it was you?' 'Because I'd be the cleverest dog you'd ever seen, and I'd do things that only you and I knew about. I'd dance, and open doors and pee in Mama's dresser drawer.'"

He laughs contentedly. Then, our hands smelling like tomato leaves, he tells me the secret again. The secret was his favorite scary story. Rei had told it to him once. He says, "Come on, let's pull weeds." And he says, "Before we lived here, a blind man lived here. But the blind man died. Then, years later, Grandpa Ton put in electricity, but every night the lights turned off on their own. In the evenings, when we'd turn on the bulbs, poof. Like someone had hit the switch. Like someone had gone through the house, room by room, and turned off all the lights. The repairmen came to have a look, but the cables were fine, and the switches were fine, and everything was the way it was supposed to be. It must have been a ghost. Then Rei said to Grandpa Ton, 'Remember, Ton, remember blind Miquel?' Miquel was one of Grandpa Ton's great-uncles, who'd died years before. When Uncle Miquel was alive, he would always walk around with his hands on the walls to feel his way and not stumble over the furniture. One stormy night, when the lights in each room of our house turned off, one after the other, poof, poof, poof, Grandpa Ton shouted, loud as thunder: 'Lift your arms, Uncle Miquel, for goodness' sake, you're hitting all the switches!' And after that shout, the lights never turned off on their own again."

And then the headlights come in through the window and wake me up.

The dream lingers like an old dried snakeskin, and I hear a car outside, and the creak-creak made by all the things that crunch under the weight of its wheels.

When I stand up, Lluna is growling low. I don't like the fact that Lluna's growling. I go over to the closet in the entryway and grab the shotgun and I'm surprised by my fear and that I've reached for the shotgun. I put on some boots, to stomp hard, because going out barefoot is like going out in a swimsuit. And I think about Hilari, who was in the vegetable patch, just a few moments ago, in my dream. And my sleepiness and the memory of Hilari weigh on me like grief. The fear wants me to wake up. The vehicle has stopped. I go out, with a jacket over my pajamas and the shotgun and the boots. The car is dark and I can't see who's inside it. I hadn't checked the time but the night is black as death and silent. It is somewhere between four and five. What the hell could they want at this hour? I don't like it. I glance over at the vegetable garden, and no one's there, Hilari's not there. Maybe I should've pretended I was sleeping, like people who are being robbed do. And I think about Oriol and his night of thieves. The headlights turn off. The front of the car is all smashed up. The door opens and I don't say anything because my tongue is tied and Lluna is in front of me, barking and barking and barking and growling, and flashing all her teeth and gnashing them together as she barks. And then a man comes out, and my heart skips a beat, because I recognize him.

From out of the car comes Jaume. I grab the dog by the neck, and I say calming words, and she barks, and barks, and I say, "Lluna, Lluna, sssshh," and the shotgun almost slips out of my hand. Jaume stands beside the car like a ghost, like an offering, and when I rise and go over to him, he looks at me with his eyes lowered, with old eyes and an old face. No, not old—swollen, and wooden. His eyes are hidden beneath the lashes and the brows, as if I were a burning fire or a setting sun. As if I could flow, molten, and scorch him. I take all the steps until I am standing in front of him, and then I say, "Do you want to come in?"

Everything around him and above him and behind him is dark, and I need to turn to get a little light into my field of vision. Air into my eyes. I look at the house so that, for a second, it seems like he's not there. Just as Hilari is not in the vegetable patch.

He follows me and the dog follows him. Lluna sniffs him and isn't barking anymore and gives him an austere welcome in the form of allowing him into the house. She will appreciate his presence because animals appreciate his presence, and Ruda always wanted him around, and dogs pass that down in their blood.

I lead him to the kitchen and he sits on the bench. The dog slides under the table and I suddenly feel like someone's removed everything inside me, intestines, and stomach, and lungs and liver and every last thing.

So Jaume doesn't disappear, and so too much light doesn't get into our eyes, which have forgotten about sleep as if they'd never be sleepy again, and so we can't see each other too well, or see all the things that've happened to us up until now, and all the years, and the pajamas I'm wearing and his dirty clothes, I get the fire going again but I don't turn on any lights.

And suddenly, Jaume is crying. He cries seated at the table, without moaning. It's hard to see, but the drops that are falling on his arms and onto the wood are round and fat, and go pling, pling. Like a leak. The dog, noticing, goes over to him and pushes her back against his calf muscles, and the animal's caress makes him cry more. At first I don't want to look at him while he cries. As if it isn't right. And I watch the embers, their red hearts. But then I think I should look at him. That crying is a good thing. And that, in fact, he owes me these few tears, and I turn to look at him.

When he dries his cheeks I make some coffee. I make coffee to keep my hands busy and to get the warm coffee into us. Because as long as you can still swallow, everything's okay. I unscrew the coffeepot and I rinse it in cold water, then fill it. I grab the package from the pantry and a teaspoon and I add the coffee, little by little until it's full. I close it up well, because if it's not well closed, it can explode. I light the burner and place the coffeepot on it and when I blow out the match, with my back still to him, I say we never blamed him, that it was an accident and we all knew that. I say it cruelly. My eyes aren't crying and have no tears welling up inside them as I say, "I lost you both at once. You and Hilari." It is a rebuke. Like a shove. Like a punch, the hardest I could deal him. With my fist closed. With my hand open and flat. With both fists at the same time. And I get the cups ready.

At first, after Hilari died, I used to imagine Jaume's release, him coming to me, destroyed, and I would receive him tenderly. We'd hug each other and cry, we'd hug and cry, and there'd be no need for me to say that I forgave him, because he'd already know, he could feel it in my body. Then, as the months passed and he refused my visits, instead I'd go see his father who was living alone up in the house, with the house falling down around him, and he ended up dying all alone, and then after a while Jaume got out, but he didn't come back, and the grief and the not understanding anything scabbed over and got so infected it took me years to clean it out. Then, if I imagined him coming or passing through and running into him up in town, I would look at him cruelly, angry, cynical, and venomous, filled with all the rage and the grief mixed together.

I get the sugar and the spoons. When the coffee boils I pour it into the cups. I place one beside his hands and I'm a little scared to sit down in front of him but I sit down anyway. He nods in a way that must mean thanks and puts two fingers over the steam that rises from the cup, which is a big one, with room for milk. And I'm losing hope. I'm losing hope because he's here and he's not saying anything. Because he's not speaking, like some old dog. Because he's waiting for me to be the one who says things, who yanks the words out of him like teeth. And then I ask, "Why did you come?"

And he answers, "I ran over a roe-deer."

His voice hasn't changed. I look at him and he lifts his eyes and our eyes meet. He has the same exact voice. My eyes fill with hot blood because he has the exact same voice. And he continues, as if a faucet had been opened, "Like the one that day with Hilari."

And it's nice that he says his name. Hilari, Hilari, Hilari, Hilari, Hilari, Hilari, Hilari, Hilari. His eyes like knives.

"Where's the roe-deer now?" I ask.

"In the car," he says.

And I don't want to. And I do want to. I get up. I'd like to stay and say more things. And for him to say more things, a lot more. But I get up. I retrace the path to the entryway and I tell myself there are important things to do, necessary things. I grab the shotgun from the table in the entryway and I go out. The night is pleasant, and I go down the stairs slowly so I won't make noise. The dog comes up behind me. When I get close to the car, it looks like a ship run aground, an abandoned house. The door Jaume left open, like a torn ear. With its snout destroyed after a fight. I approach it stealthily. The windowpanes look at me black as water. I approach the open door and inside everything is dark, and I can't really see the seats, and I focus my eyes on the blackness and nothing is moving. I have the shotgun ready in my right hand, but there's nothing inside the car. I lower my head and I put my hands on the footrest and nothing. Just a bitter, strong, stinky smell of wild animal and beer and blood and some other rough thing.

I hear Jaume walking from the house. I keep moving my hands along the floor of the car and I feel dampness and then I pull them out and I can't see what color it is and I wipe them on my leg, and Jaume, who is beside me by then, says, "I'm sorry."

I know that already, that you're sorry, but I don't say anything, because it's good that you're sorry. Because you should be sorry about a number of things.

"Do you have a list of all the things you're sorry about?" I ask.

He smiles a little, as if it hurt to smile. And then, "I'm sorry for the accident," he says. "I'm sorry that it was my fault Hilari died. I'm sorry for being too afraid to come to you and say I was sorry. I'm sorry for not wanting you to see me like that. I'm sorry for leaving and not coming back and not telling you that I loved you, or that I wanted you, or anything. I'm sorry I didn't have the guts."

Then I flare up. Angry as a mountain, I respond, shotgun in hand, "I'm sorry you didn't come back and I'm sorry for always wanting you to come back. And I'm sorry that it was your fault Hilari died and how that destroyed everything. And I'm sorry for forgiving you, when I forgive you. And I'm sorry for not forgiving you, when I don't forgive you. And I'm sorry that sometimes being sorry's not enough, like how sometimes loving's not enough."

And then I walk toward the house. I go put the shotgun in the closet. I'd like to go look for the roe-deer. For the sun not to come up. For the round moon to stay in the garden, move in like a pregnant cat. For Jaume to stay in the garden, move in like a pregnant cat. For us to be able to try to say all the things many times. The sad cups are still on the table in the kitchen, in the dark, and the dog goes to the bedroom because it's time to sleep. Because we were sleeping before and he woke us up and now it seems like this night is never going to end. But I don't want to go to sleep. I don't want Jaume to leave. With everything there is to say.

I go back outside with empty hands and I close the front door. I sit down on the second step in front of the house, beneath the open sky and beneath the dark night and beneath the round moon. I signal with my head for Jaume, who's still by the car, to come over. He does, and he sits down next to me, and under his smell of beer and sweat, I get a terrible whiff filled with memories. I want us to go look for the roe-deer. I want us to look for it tomorrow when the sun comes up and not find it. I want it to have run all night. To be running still. To hide so we'll have to look for it for years.

I extend an open hand, so he'll put his immense hand on top of mine. So gently that our fingertips barely touch.

"I want you to tell me everything," I say. "Starting with Hilari and the accident and then all the rest, and prison. And what you're doing now. And if you don't want to tell me, or you don't know how to tell me, I want you to leave."

He nods his head.

"And then I'll tell you everything," I continue.

Each and every one of the things. And when we're done, we'll see who we are.

"I bought the butcher's shop," I say all of a sudden, just blurting it out. And he squeezes my outstretched hand, like he's hugging it with his immense paw.

"I thought I would come and you wouldn't want to see me," he says. "I imagined your kids but I couldn't see their faces. Are you okay out here?"

Some things can't be said inside houses.

"How can you forgive me for the last twenty-five years?" he asks suddenly.

I don't answer and I don't glance at him but I know his expression. He's got grief on his face and resignation. He's got a pained face and the face of a wet dog and I look at him quickly out of the corner of my eye and he's got the expression I knew he would have. I let my eyes turn toward the trees in front of the house.

"How can you forgive me?"

Some birds are singing the daybreak, but it's still black night. Shush, I think, it's too early for that. He is silent and focuses on the darkness, farther out, on the leaves and the branches, dark as the throat of a wolf, as the throat of a dog.

And now he'll say some things. Things that lead steadily from one to the next, like beads on a string. The ones he remembers, the ones that light up like firecrackers when it's time to say them and you're able to say them. The ones that have to be pulled out, like onions. The ones that have to be said softly and the ones that have to be said little by little. The ones that burn. The ones that have to be said looking at the trees, and the ones that have to be said looking at the grass, the ones that have to be said looking at our hands, one on top of the other, and then looking at me. And I will listen. Then I'll say some things. The ones I can. And then the day will break. First gray, then blue, and then yellow.

AUTHOR'S NOTE

I first discovered many of the legends that appear in this book in *Muntanyes maleïdes* by Pep Coll.

In order to write "The Names of the Women" I read about witches and witch trials in *Orígens i evolució de la cacera de bruixes a Catalunya* by Pau Castell Granados and also in *Un judici de bruixes a la Catalunya del Barroc: L'esquirol 1619–1621* by Jaume Crosas Casadesús.

The character of Eva, the Republican girl, was inspired by the little girl in a photograph of the Gracia Bamala family, which was first published on February 18, 1939, in the French magazine *L'illustration*, as part of a feature story on the Republican exile titled "La tragédie espagnole, sur la frontière des Pyrénées," whose authorship is unclear. When creating her story, I also relied on the transcript of the documentary *Ni perdono, ni oblido* by Joan Giralt Filella.

And finally, the chapter "The Bear" would not be what it is if Joan-Lluís Lluís hadn't written *El dia de l'ós*. And "Crunch" would not be what it is if Mikel Aboitiz hadn't written the story "Fundación mítica de Islandia" for the project *Notes on a Novel (That I Am Not Going to Write), or The Swimming Pool, or the Hair, the Herb and the Bread or the Tomato Plant*.

ACKNOWLEDGMENTS

Endless thanks to Oscar, my mother and father, Marta Garolera, Lluís Calvo, Irene Jaular, Lluís Bassaganya, Pol Ordeig, Xavier Castellana, Alexandra Laudo, Jan Ferrarons, and Mikel Aboitiz.